Frederic P. Miller, Agnes F. Vandome,
John McBrewster (Ed.)

LZ 127 Graf Zeppelin

Frederic P. Miller, Agnes F. Vandome, John McBrewster (Ed.)

LZ 127 Graf Zeppelin

Airship, Ferdinand von Zeppelin, Graf, Hugo Eckener, Maybach, Buoyancy compensator (aviation), LZ 130 Graf Zeppelin, List of Zeppelins

Alphascript Publishing

Imprint

Permission is granted to copy, distribute and/or modify this document under the terms of the GNU Free Documentation License, Version 1.2 or any later version published by the Free Software Foundation; with no Invariant Sections, with the Front-Cover Texts, and with the Back-Cover Texts. A copy of the license is included in the section entitled "GNU Free Documentation License".

All parts of this book are extracted from Wikipedia, the free encyclopedia (www.wikipedia.org).

You can get detailed informations about the authors of this collection of articles at the end of this book. The editors (Ed.) of this book are no authors. They have not modified or extended the original texts.

Pictures published in this book can be under different licences than the GNU Free Documentation License. You can get detailed informations about the authors and licences of pictures at the end of this book.

The content of this book was generated collaboratively by volunteers. Please be advised that nothing found here has necessarily been reviewed by people with the expertise required to provide you with complete, accurate or reliable information. Some information in this book maybe misleading or wrong. The Publisher does not guarantee the validity of the information found here. If you need specific advice (f.e. in fields of medical, legal, financial, or risk management questions) please contact a professional who is licensed or knowledgeable in that area.

Any brand names and product names mentioned in this book are subject to trademark, brand or patent protection and are trademarks or registered trademarks of their respective holders. The use of brand names, product names, common names, trade names, product descriptions etc. even without a particular marking in this works is in no way to be construed to mean that such names may be regarded as unrestricted in respect of trademark and brand protection legislation and could thus be used by anyone.

Cover image: www.PureStockX.com
Concerning the licence of the cover image please contact PureStockX.

Publisher:
Alphascript Publishing is a trademark of
VDM Publishing House Ltd.,17 Rue Meldrum, Beau Bassin,1713-01 Mauritius
Email: info@vdm-publishing-house.com
Website: www.vdm-publishing-house.com

Published in 2009

Printed in: U.S.A., U.K., Germany. This book was not produced in Mauritius.

ISBN: 978-613-0-21976-5

Contents

Articles

LZ 127 Graf Zeppelin	1
Airship	13
Ferdinand von Zeppelin	34
Graf	39
Hugo Eckener	43
Maybach	49
Buoyancy compensator (aviation)	53
LZ 130 Graf Zeppelin	57
List of Zeppelins	63

References

Article Sources and Contributors	75
Image Sources, Licenses and Contributors	76

LZ 127 Graf Zeppelin

LZ 127 *Graf Zeppelin*

Role	Passenger airship
National origin	Germany
Manufacturer	Luftschiffbau Zeppelin
Designed by	Ludwig Dürr
First flight	18 September 1928
Retired	18 June 1937
Status	Scrapped March 1940
Number built	1

LZ 127 *Graf Zeppelin* (Deutsches Luftschiff Zeppelin #127; Registration: **D-LZ 127**) was a large German passenger carrying rigid → airship which operated commercially from 1928 to 1937. It was named after the German pioneer of airships, → Ferdinand von Zeppelin, who held the rank of → Graf or Count in the German nobility. During its operating life the great airship made 590 flights covering more than a million miles.

Design and development

The LZ 127 was originally planned to exploit the latest technology in airships, building on the advances of the earlier LZ126. → Dr. Hugo Eckener had to campaign for its construction and only after two years of lobbying did that proceed at the Zeppelin works, Luftschiffbau Zeppelin, at Friedrichshafen in Germany.

The *Graf Zeppelin* flew for the first time on 18 September 1928[1] and, with a total length of 236.6 metres (776 ft) and volume of 105000 cubic metres (3700000 cu ft), was the largest airship up to that time. It was powered by five → Maybach 550 horsepower (410 kW) engines[1] that could burn either Blau gas or gasoline[2]. The ship achieved a maximum speed of 128 kilometres per hour (80 mph, 70 knots) operating at total maximum thrust of 2650 horsepower (1980 kW), which reduced to the normal cruising speed of 117 km/h (73 mph, 63 knots) when running with normal thrust of 2150 horsepower (1600 kW), ignoring wind speeds.[2] Some flights were made using only Blau gas, and for this purpose 12 gas cells were used with a total volume up to 30,000 cubic metres. That amount allowed around 100 hours at cruising speed. The fuel tank had a maximum capacity for 67 hours cruise. Using both gasoline and Blau gas could give 118 hours cruise.

Construction of the *Graf Zeppelin* in Friedrichshafen: the lower and middle gangways are highlighted green with main rings in red; two people are shown in yellow.

Generally the *"Graf Zeppelin"* had a usable payload capacity of 15,000 kilograms for a 10,000 kilometres cruise.[2]

Initially it was to be used for experimental and demonstration purposes to prepare the way for regular airship traveling, but also carried passengers and mail to cover the costs.

Two small ram air turbines attached to the main gondola on swinging arms generated supplemental electricity: one for the radio room, the other for passenger lighting, the galley appliances, and as a reserve. Accumulators stored the electrical energy produced so that radio operation was independent of airspeed.[3] The main electricity generating plant was located inside the hull comprising two fuel-burning generators.[4] The gondola also had a gasoline-fueled emergency generator.

Gondola layout

Behind the front command cabin through a door lay the map room, with two large open access hatches to allow the command crew to communicate with the navigators. From the map room ascending a ladder allowed access to a keel corridor inside the hull. The map room had two large windows, one on each side. A rear door led from the map room to a central corridor with the three-man radio room to the left and the electric kitchen to the right, and a short passage to the main entrance-exit door on the right (when facing front). The corridor ended at a door that opened into the main dining and sitting room, with four large windows. At the rear of this room a door opened into the long corridor to access the passenger's cabins and washrooms and toilet facilities.[1] Each passenger cabin by day was set with a sofa which by night the crew would convert to two beds, one above the other.[4] The crew's quarters were inside the hull reached by a catwalk. The kitchen was equipped with a single electric oven with two compartments and hot plates on top.[4]

Radio equipment

Many people were needed to hold down the D-LZ127. The red circle indicates the ram air turbine electric generator just under the radio room window.

The Graf's radio room was outfitted with the most modern radio equipment for an airship at the time.[3] Three radio officers served there communicating with ground stations and ships, performing radio navigation,[3] receiving weather reports as well as sending private telegrams for passengers.[5] A one kilowatt valve transmitter (about 140 Watt antenna power) was used to send telegrams over the longwave band of 500 to 3,000 metre.[3] An emergency transmitter with 70 Watt antenna power was available for both telegraph and radio telephone, using 300 to 1,300 metre wavelengths, powered either by the accumulator or the gasoline generator.[3]

The main antenna comprised two 120 metre long wires, with lead weights at their ends. They could be lowered by electric motor or hand crank. The emergency antenna was a 40 metre wire stretched from a ring on the airship hull.[3] Three high quality receivers, each with six valves, served the wavelength ranges 120 to 1,200 metre (Medium frequency), 400 to 4,000 metre (Low frequency) and 3,000 to 25,000 metre (overlapping Low frequency and Very low frequency).[3] Additionally the room had a shortwave receiver for wavelengths 10 to 280 metre (High frequency).[3]

A modern direction finder, as was then used for radio navigation in large passenger ships, used a steerable ring antenna to determine the airship's position from any two radio transmitters either land or ship-based.[3] During the airship's transatlantic flight to the United States in October 1928, the radio room sent 484 private telegrams and 160 press telegrams.[3]

Operational history

From its first flight on 18 September 1928 until its last flight on 18 June 1937, the Graf saw nearly nine years of uninterrupted service, totaling nearly two years in the air and traveling 1.7 million kilometres.[6] Its seventh flight was its first Atlantic crossing,[7] thereafter it made regular flights across the South Atlantic to Brazil, one round the world tour, a polar expedition, two roundtrips to the Middle East, and a few within Europe. While the *Graf Zeppelin* only visited the United States five times (twice during the "Round the World Flight"), the airship made a total of 64 flights to South America.

Tower of Zeppelin, in Recife, Brazil

Graf Zeppelin in Helsinki, Finland.

First intercontinental passenger airship flight

Flown ppc from the First North American Flight of the D-LZ127 1928

Dr. Eckener commanded the "Graf Zeppelin" on its first intercontinental trip, a transatlantic crossing which left Friedrichshafen, Germany, at 07:54 on 11 October 1928, and arrived in the United States at NAS Lakehurst, New Jersey, on 15 October after having traveled 9,926 km in 111 hours. Notwithstanding the heavy headwinds and stormy weather that slowed the journey, Eckener had nevertheless repeated the success of his first transatlantic crossing made four years earlier in October 1924, to deliver the D-LZ126 (renamed the USS Los Angeles) to the U.S. Navy. Eckener and the crew were welcomed enthusiastically with a "ticker tape" parade in New York the next day and a subsequent invitation to the White House.

This first transatlantic trip was not without its difficulties, however, as the airship suffered potentially serious damage to its port tail fin on the third day of the flight when a large section of the linen covering was ripped loose while passing through a mid-ocean squall line. With the engines stopped, the ship's riggers did their best to tie down the torn fabric to the framework and sew blankets to the ship's envelope while attempting to not fall to the raging seas just below. In the interest of safety, the riggers (Who included Dr. Eckener's son, Knut) retreated back into the ship whenever it dropped to within a couple of hundred feet of the ocean's surface. This allowed the engines to be restarted to maintain lift.[8] The Graf crossed the U.S. coast at Cape Charles, Virginia, around 10 AM on 15 October, passed over Washington, D.C., at 12:20 PM, Baltimore, MD, at 1 PM, Philadelphia, PA, at 2:40 PM, New York City at 4 PM, and landed at NAS Lakehurst at 5:38 PM.[9]

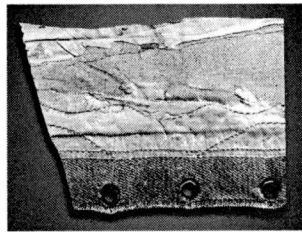

A portion of the damaged fabric covering removed from the "Graf Zeppelin" in October 1928, after its first transatlantic flight from Germany to NAS Lakehurst, NJ.

In addition to the passengers and crew, there was also a stowaway on the flight, 19-year old Clarence Terhune, who had secreted himself onboard the *Graf Zeppelin* in Lakehurst, New Jersey.[10] He appears in a Gaumont Graphic Newsreel working for his passage in the airship's kitchen. Terhune was returned to the U.S. on the French liner SS Ile de France along with a number of airship crewmembers.[11] [12] [13]

The "interrupted flight"

Flown cover autographed by the "Graf Zeppelin's" commander, Dr. Hugo Eckener from the nearly disastrous 1929 "Interrupted Flight".

While the "Graf Zeppelin" would eventually have a safe and highly successful nine-year career, the airship was almost lost just a half a year after its maiden flight while attempting to make its second trip to the United States in May 1929. Shortly after dark on 16 May, the first night of the flight ("1. Amerikafahrt 1929"), the airship lost two of its five engines while over the Mediterranean off the southwest coast of Spain forcing Dr. Eckener to abandon the trip and return to Friedrichshafen. While flying up the Rhône Valley in France against a stiff headwind the next afternoon, however, two of the remaining three engines also failed and the airship began to be pushed backwards toward the sea.

As Dr. Eckener desperately looked for a suitable place to crash land the airship, the French Air Ministry advised him that he would be permitted to land at the Naval Airship Base at Cuers-Pierrefeu about ten miles from Toulon to use the mooring mast and hangar of the lost airship *Dixmude* (France's only dirigible which crashed in the Mediterranean in 1923 resulting in the loss of 52 lives) if the Graf could reach the facility before being blown out to sea. Although barely able to control the Graf on its one remaining engine, Eckener managed to make a difficult but successful emergency night landing at Cuers.[14] After making temporary repairs, the Graf finally returned to Friedrichshafen on 24 May. Mail carried on the flight received a one-line cachet reading *"Delivery delayed due to cancelation of the 1st America trip"* and was held at Friedrichshafen until 1 August 1929, when the airship made another attempt to cross the Atlantic for Lakehurst arriving on 4 August 1929. Four days later, the "Graf Zeppelin" departed Lakehurst for another daring enterprise — a complete circumnavigation of the globe.

Round-the-world flight

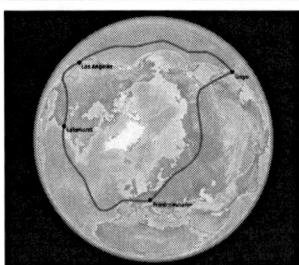

Route of Graf Zeppelin's round the world flight.
Click each globe in turn:Germany:47°39'14"N 9°28'44"E47.654°N 9.479°E [15] 47°39'14"N 9°28'44"E47.654°N 9.479°E [16]
USA:40°01'59"N 74°21'13"W40.033°N 74.3536°W [17] 40°01'59"N 74°21'13"W40.033°N 74.3536°W [18]
Germany:47°39'14"N 9°28'44"E47.654°N 9.479°E [19] Japan:36°03'00"N 140°13'01"E36.05°N 140.217°E [20]
36°03'00"N 140°13'01"E36.05°N 140.217°E [21] USA:33°56'33"N 118°24'29"W33.9425°N 118.408°W [22] 33°56'33"N
118°24'29"W33.9425°N 118.408°W [23] 41°52'03"N 87°37'27"W41.8675°N 87.6243°W [24] 40°01'59"N
74°21'13"W40.033°N 74.3536°W [25]
Germany:47°39'14"N 9°28'44"E47.654°N 9.479°E [26]

Cover flown on the "Graf Zeppelin" from Lakehurst to Lakehurst on the "Round-the-World" flight, 8 August - 4 September 1929

The growing popularity of the "giant of the air" made it easy for Zeppelin company chief → Dr. Hugo Eckener to find sponsors for a "Round-the-World" flight. One of these was the American press tycoon William Randolph Hearst, who requested the tour to officially start at Lakehurst Naval Air Station, NJ.[27] As with the October 1928 flight to New York, Hearst had placed a reporter, Grace Marguerite Hay Drummond-Hay, on board,[27] who thereby became the first woman to circumnavigate the globe by air.

Starting there on 8 August 1929, *Graf Zeppelin* flew back across the Atlantic to Friedrichshafen to refuel before continuing on August 15 across the vastness of Siberia to Tokyo (Kasumigaura Naval Air Station), a nonstop leg of 6988 miles (11246 km), arriving three days later on 18 August.[7] Dr. Eckener believed that some of the lands they crossed in Siberia had never before been seen by modern explorers. After staying in Tokyo for five days, on 23 August, the *Graf Zeppelin* continued across the Pacific to California flying first over San Francisco before heading south to stop at Mines Field in Los Angeles for the first ever nonstop flight of any kind across the Pacific Ocean. The Pacific leg was 5998 miles (9653 km) and took three days.[7] The airship's final leg across the United States took it over Chicago before landing back at Lakehurst NAS on 29 August, taking two days and covering 2996 miles (4822 km).[7] [28]

The flying time for the Lakehurst to Lakehurst legs was 12 days and 11 minutes.[7] The entire voyage took 21 days, 5 hours and 31 minutes including the initial and final trips between Friedrichshafen and NAS Lakehurst during which time the airship travelled 49,618 km (30,831 miles) whereas the distance covered on the designated "Round the World" portion from Lakehurst to Lakehurst was 31,400 km (19,500 miles). One of Hearst's guests on board was the newlywed couple; the Arctic explorer Sir Hubert Wilkins and his bride Suzanne Bennett. The trip was given to them as a wedding gift.

A U.S. franked letter carried on the whole trip from Lakehurst to Lakehurst required $3.55 USD in postage, the equivalent in 2007 of roughly $43 if based on the CPI.[29]

Silver 3 Reichsmark coin (1930 A) honoring the "Graf Zeppelin's" "Round the World" flight (Weltflug 1929).

The polar flight

Flown USSR ppc delivered by the "Graf Zeppelin" to the Soviet icebreaker "Malygin" on the "Polar Flight" 1931

The ship pursued another spectacular destination in July 1931 with a research trip to the Arctic; this had already been a dream of Count Zeppelin 20 years earlier, which could not, however, be realized at the time due to the outbreak of war.

In July 1930, Hugo Eckener had already piloted the Graf on a three-day trip to Norway and Spitsbergen, in order to determine its performance in this region. Shortly after Eckener made a three day flight to Iceland, both trips completed without technical problems.[5]

The initial idea was to rendezvous with the ill-fated *Nautilus*, the submarine of polar researcher George Hubert Wilkins, who was attempting a trip under the ice. This plan was abandoned when the U-boat encountered recurring technical problems, leading to its eventual scuttling in a Bergen fjord.[30]

Eckener instead began to plan a rendezvous with a surface vessel. He intended funding to be secured by delivering mail post to the ship. After advertising, around fifty thousand letters were collected from around the world weighing a total of about 300 kilograms. The rendezvous vessel, the Russian icebreaker Malygin, on which the Italian airshipman and polar explorer Umberto Nobile was a guest, required another 120 kilograms of post. The major costs of the expedition were met solely by sale of postage stamps.[5] The rest of the funding came from Aeroarctic and the Ullstein-Verlag in exchange for exclusive reporting rights.

The 1931 polar flight took one week from 24 July 1931 until the 31st. The Graf traveled about 10,600 kilometres, the longest leg without refueling was 8,600 kilometres. The average speed was 88 km/h.

Route:

- Friedrichshafen–Berlin – 600 km in 8 hours (75 km/h)
- Berlin–Leningrad – 1,400 km in 16 hours (87 km/h)
- Leningrad–Kanin – 1,300 km in 12 hours (108 km/h)
- Kanin–Franz-Joseph-Land – 1,200 km in 18 hours (67 km/h)
- Franz-Joseph-Land–Nordland–Taimyr–Novaya Zemlya – 2,400 km in 32 hours (75 km/h)
- Novaya Zemlya–Leningrad – 2,300 km in 25 hours (92 km/h)
- Leningrad–Berlin – 1,400 km in 13 hours (108 km/h)
- Berlin–Friedrichshafen – 600 km in 8 hours (75 km/h)[5]

Germany issued this stamp commemorating the Graf polar trip

Goals:

- Test the Graf Zeppelin under Arctic conditions
- scientific and geographic research of large areas of the Arctic
  - measurement of magnetic field changes
  - meteorological measurements (including weather balloon launches)
  - geo-photographic recording of large areas with a panoramic camera (that would take years if by ship or by land)

All participants were satisfied after the trip: the airship demonstrated its usefulness in the Arctic.

Middle East flights

Flown ppc carried on the D-LZ 127 "Graf Zeppelin" to Syria on the "Mittelmeerfahrt 1929"

The "Graf Zeppelin" made two visits to the Middle East during its career. The first took place over four days in April 1929, without landing but during which mail was dropped to the large German colony at Jaffa in Palestine. The second flight took place in 1931 beginning on 9 April with a flight to Cairo, Egypt, where the airship landed less than two days later. After a brief stop the "Graf Zeppelin" proceeded on to Palestine before returning to Friedrichshafen on 23 April, just an hour over four days after departure. The trip took 97 hours, covered 9,000 kilometres and crossed 14 countries on three continents. The highlights were:

- Launched 9 April at 06:10, following the Rhone valley and over Corsica, Sardinia, Sicily, and Malta. By 05:15 the following morning Graf reached the African coast at Tripoli near Bengasi, then on towards Alexandria, the Bucht von Sollum at 09:00, flying over Alexandria at 13:00, following the Nile towards Cairo.
- Flew 200 metres over the Giza pyramid complex, over the Pyramid of Cheops, then following the Nile towards Heluan. Late evening reached the pyramid of Saqqara.
- Nightflight northwards along the Nile towards Damietta.
- 11 April at 5:15 landed at Almaza (Almasy) airfield near Cairo. British air force soldiers comprising the ground crew. Thirty thousand curious onlookers must be held back with fire hoses.
- After a short stayover, relaunched eastwards over the Suez canal and the bight of Gaza, 10:00 arriving in Jerusalem
- 100 metres over the Church of the Holy Sepulchre the engines were stopped and the ship floated "still" for several minutes.
- Fly over Shechem, Emmaus, the limestone mountains over the desert, 16:00 arrived at Cairo, 17:00 landed at Almaza, half hour stayover, resuming flying towards Siwa Oasis, (Libyan Desert). In the desert villages, many people fled into their huts before the airship.

One image of a stereoscopic pair made while the Graf flew over the pyramids (click to access the full pair)

- Night: the airship crossed over Tripoli, by morning it was over Crete, then along the Albanian coast towards towards Split in Dalmatia. The ship flew 1700 metres over the Karst hills. By 21:30 Agram in Yugoslavia, midnight Vienna, Passau, Augsburg, Ulm
- 7:00 lands at Friedrichshafen.[5]

Golden age

Zeppelin passenger lapel pins

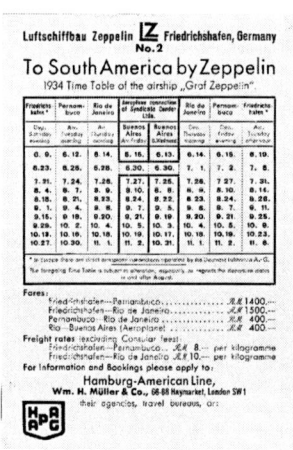

Schedule of 1934 Flights to South America

Cover carried on the First 1934 South America Flight of the 10 flown that season.

The *Graf Zeppelin* undertook a number of trips around Europe, and following a successful tour to South America in May 1930, it was decided to open the first regular transatlantic airship line, traveling mainly from Germany to Brazil (64 such round trips overall) with occasional stops, among them Spain, Miami,[31] London,[32] and Berlin.[33] At one of the Berlin visits a glider that was released from under its hull performed a loop in front of cheering crowds,[34] and on one of the Brazil trips British Pathé News filmed on board.[35].

Almost every flight had a reporter on board, who would radio a report to the ground via Morse Code. Such articles made Lady Drummond-Hay famous, and she would be pictured in advertisements featuring the Graf.[36]

In October 1933, the *Graf Zeppelin* made an appearance at the Century of Progress World's Fair in Chicago, after circling over the fair,[37] then landing and relaunching 25 minutes later. Despite the beginning of the Great Depression and growing competition by fixed-wing aircraft, D-LZ127 would transport an increasing number of passengers and mail across the ocean every year until 1937. Post and cargo provided most of the income for operating the Graf. In one transatlantic flight the Graf would carry 52,000 postcards and 50,000 letters, and by its last flight it had carried 53 tonnes of mail. Since 1912 Zeppelins were allowed to postmark and sort mail onboard and the Graf managed to deliver South America-bound about a week faster than by ship.[38] However in general the Deutsche Zeppelin Reederei made a loss each year. When the Hindenburg entered service in 1936 prospects became better and a profit was expected for 1937 by delivering mail on both it and the Graf, but the *Hindenburg's* loss in May 1937 put an end to all commercial Zeppelin service.[39]

Successor abandoned

Dr. Eckener intended to supplement the successful craft by another, similar Zeppelin, projected as D-LZ128. However the disastrous accident of the British passenger airship *R101* in 1931 led the Zeppelin company to reconsider the safety of hydrogen-filled vessels, and the design was abandoned in favor of a new project. D-LZ129, which was to eventually be named the *Hindenburg*, would advance Zeppelin technology considerably and was intended to be filled with helium.

After the Hindenburg disaster the story arose that an embargo imposed by the United States because of the looming war prevented German access to the required large quantities of helium, leading to the conversion of the Hindenburg to a hydrogen design. However it is now known that Eckener successfully visited President Roosevelt himself, who promised to supply helium, but only for peaceful purposes. But after the annexation of Austria in March 1938, U.S. Secretary of the Interior Harold Ickes refused to supply helium, and the → *Graf Zeppelin II* was ultimately inflated with hydrogen. It has been suggested that the use of helium was ruled out on financial grounds.

End of an era

After the *Hindenburg* disaster in 1937, public faith in the safety of dirigibles was shattered, and flying passengers in hydrogen-filled vessels became untenable. D-LZ127 *Graf Zeppelin* was retired one month past the disaster and turned into a museum. The end for the *Graf Zeppelin* came with the outbreak of World War II. In March 1940, Hermann Göring, the German Air Minister *(Reichsluftfahrtminister)*, ordered the destruction of the remaining dirigibles, and the duralumin parts were fed into the German war industry.

Legacy

During its career, the ship flew more than one and half million kilometres (thus becoming the first aircraft in history to fly over a million miles), 590 flights, and made 144 ocean crossings (143 across the Atlantic, one across the Pacific) carrying 13,110 passengers[6] with a perfect passenger safety record, making it the most successful rigid airship ever built.[1]

US Air Mail stamp (C-13), issued April 1930

As evidence of how it caught the imagination of the world, a number of countries issued postage stamps either commemorating flights of the Zeppelin or for use on this (and later) airships. Some are fairly common, others quite rare. A considerable number of covers (envelopes) carried on flights still exist and are avidly collected. In addition, a board game was made in its name[40].

Specifications

General characteristics

- **Crew:** 40
- **Capacity:** 20 passengers
- **Length:** 236.53 m (776 ft 0 in)
- **Diameter:** 30.48 m (100 ft 0 in)
- **Volume:** 105,000 m³ (3,700,000 ft³)
- **Useful lift:** 60,000 kg (132,000 lb)
- **Powerplant:** 5 × → Maybach engines, 410 kW (550 hp) each

Performance

- **Maximum speed:** 128 km/h (80 mph)

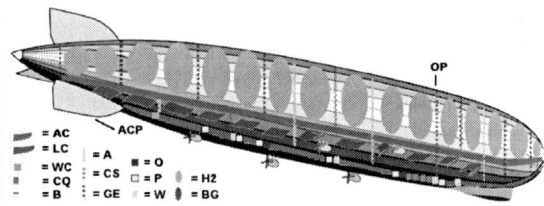

internal components and gas cell locations shown schematically, excluding passenger and engine gondolas. Key: ACP = Auxiliary control post red = AC = axial corridor running from main ring -2 to the front mooring hub blue = LC = lower corridor running from main ring 20 to ring 211 ending at ladder to axial corridor orange = WC = crew's toilet beige = CQ = crew's quarters with tables, chairs and berths beige = B = berths or cargo space blue stripes = A = ventilation shaft green stripes = CS = climbing shaft brown stripes GE = exhaust gas shaft brown box = O = oil tanks yellow box = P = petrol tanks light blue box = W = water tank OP = Observation post on top of hull pink cell = H2 = hydrogen gas cell magenta cell = BG = Blaugas cell

See also

- → Buoyancy compensator (aviation)
- → D-LZ130 Graf Zeppelin II

Related lists

- → List of Zeppelins

References

Bibliography

- Archbold, Rick. *Hindenburg: An Illustrated History.* Toronto: Viking Studio/Madison Press, 1994. ISBN 0-670-85225-2.
- Bomberguy. Graf Zeppelin [41] Bomberguy Aviation History, selected clips. Retrieved: 11 June 2008.
- Botting, Douglas. *Dr. Eckener's Dream Machine: The Great Zeppelin and the Dawn of Air Travel.* New York: Henry Holt & Co., 2001. ISBN 0-80506-458-3.
- Brewer, G. Daniel. *Hydrogen Aircraft Technology.* Boca Raton, Florida: CRC Press, 1991. ISBN 0-84935-838-8.
- Busch, Heinrich. "Funkverkehr auf dem Luftschiff LZ 127 Graf Zeppelin". [42] (in German), 14 August 2006. Retrieved: 5 July 2008.
- Dick, Harold G. and Douglas H. Robinson. *The Golden Age of the Great Passenger Airships Graf Zeppelin & Hindenburg.* Washington, D.C. and London: Smithsonian Institution Press, 1985. ISBN 1-56098-219-5.
- Duggan, John. *LZ 129 "Hindenburg": The Complete Story.* Ickenham, UK: Zeppelin Study Group, 2002. ISBN 0-9514114-8-9.
- Geisenheyner, Max. *Mit 'Graf Zeppelin' Um Die Welt: Ein Bild-Buch.* Frankfurt am Mein, Germany: Frankfurter Societäts-Druckerei G.m.b.H., 1929.
- "Honors to Dr. Hugo Eckener: The First Airship Flight Around the World." *National Geographic Magazine* Vol. LVII, No. 6, June 1930, pp. 653–688.
- Lehmann, Ernst. *Zeppelin: The Story of Lighter-than-air Craft.* London: Longmans, Green and Co., 1937.
- Puget Sound Airship Society. *Zeppelin Airships 1918-1940,* 2007. [43] Retrieved: 5 July 2008.
- Scherz, Walter. *Bau und Einrichtung des Luftschiffes "Graf Zeppelin"* (in German)- LZ127 in construction [44] JADU 2003. Retrieved: 2 June 2008.

External links

- Photographs of interior and exterior of Graf Zeppelin [45]
- Private photographs of Graf Zeppelin over Chicago's World's Fair, 1933 [46]
- The Graf Zeppelin [47], courtesy of Bomberguy [48]
- "The history and building of the Zeppelin" (Dutch) (youtube video, 5 minutes). *Nyo Visuals [Elsbeth van Noppen* [49]*. Retrieved: 20 February 2009.]*
- "Graf Zeppelin ends world flight." (1 minute 17 seconds video: aeroplane escort, Lakehurst hangar). *Universal Newspaper Newsreel.* Retrieved: 20 February 2009. [50]

References

[1] Puget Sound Airship Society 2007
[2] Scherz 2003
[3] Busch 2006
[4] Pilot und Luftschiff. LZ 127 Graf Zeppelin : Bilder aus dem Luftschiff (http://www.pilotundluftschiff.de/Galerie001.htm) (Photograph *Elektrozentrale*)
[5] wikipedia.de (2008)
[6] Brewer 1991, p. 2.
[7] Michel, Carolyn. Round-the-World Flights (http://www.wingnet.org/rtw/rtw001j.htm)
[8] Vaeth, J. Gordon. "Graf Zeppelin: The Adventures Of An Aerial Globetrotter". New York: Harper & Brothers, 1958. Library Of Congress catalogue number 58-6164
[9] "Zeppelin Safe at Lakehurst after 111-Hour Flight; Soars Over the White House and then Over New York; Moored to Mast till Wind Drops at 2 A.M.; Now in Hangar" *The New York Times*, 16 October 1928.
[10] *Air Stowaway's Own Story*, The San Antonio Light, 2 November 1928.
[11] "First Stowaway Home From Germany." *The New York Times*, 14 November 1928.
[12] GAUMONT GRAPHIC NEWSREEL (REUTERS) (1928). " TRANSPORT: Graf Zeppelin airship record trip stops off in Friedrichshafen with stowaway Clarence Terhune onboard (http://www.itnsource.com/shotlist//BHC_RTV/1928/01/01/BGT407131213/)". ITN Source. . Retrieved 2009-08-19.
[13] "Big Flight". (http://www.time.com/time/magazine/article/0,9171,846291-2,00.html) *Time*, 11 March 1929.
[14] "Zeppelin Battles Gale to Safety; Reaches Cuers, France, on One Motor; Eckener and Crew Avert Disaster" *The New York Times*, 18 May 1929.
[15] http://stable.toolserver.org/geohack/geohack.php?pagename=LZ_127_Graf_Zeppelin&params=47.654_N_9. 479_E_region:DE_type:airport_scale:1000000&title=Friedrichshafen
[16] http://stable.toolserver.org/geohack/geohack.php?pagename=LZ_127_Graf_Zeppelin&params=47.654_N_9. 479_E_region:DE_type:city_scale:10000000
[17] http://stable.toolserver.org/geohack/geohack.php?pagename=LZ_127_Graf_Zeppelin&params=40.033_N_-74. 3536_E_region:US_type:airport_scale:10000000&title=Lakehurst
[18] http://stable.toolserver.org/geohack/geohack.php?pagename=LZ_127_Graf_Zeppelin&params=40.033_N_-74. 3536_E_region:US_type:airport_scale:200000&title=Lakehurst+NAS
[19] http://stable.toolserver.org/geohack/geohack.php?pagename=LZ_127_Graf_Zeppelin&params=47.654_N_9. 479_E_region:DE_type:airport_scale:1000000&title=Friedrichshafen+refueling
[20] http://stable.toolserver.org/geohack/geohack.php?pagename=LZ_127_Graf_Zeppelin&params=36.05_N_140. 217_E_region:JP_type:airport_scale:10000000&title=Kasumigaura+Naval+Air+Base
[21] http://stable.toolserver.org/geohack/geohack.php?pagename=LZ_127_Graf_Zeppelin&params=36.05_N_140. 217_E_region:JP_type:airport_scale:1000000
[22] http://stable.toolserver.org/geohack/geohack.php?pagename=LZ_127_Graf_Zeppelin&params=33.9425_N_-118. 408_E_region:US_type:airport_scale:10000000&title=Los+Angeles
[23] http://stable.toolserver.org/geohack/geohack.php?pagename=LZ_127_Graf_Zeppelin&params=33.9425_N_-118. 408_E_region:US_type:airport_scale:400000&title=Mines+Field+LA
[24] http://stable.toolserver.org/geohack/geohack.php?pagename=LZ_127_Graf_Zeppelin&params=41.8675_N_-87. 6243_E_region:US-IL_type:city_scale:10000000&title=Chicago
[25] http://stable.toolserver.org/geohack/geohack.php?pagename=LZ_127_Graf_Zeppelin&params=40.033_N_-74. 3536_E_region:US_type:airport_scale:10000000&title=Lakehurst+NAS+second+landing
[26] http://stable.toolserver.org/geohack/geohack.php?pagename=LZ_127_Graf_Zeppelin&params=47.654_N_9. 479_E_region:DE_type:airport_scale:10000000&title=Friedrichshafen+second+and+final+landing
[27] . "Los Angeles to Lakehurst." (http://www.time.com/time/magazine/article/0,9171,737828,00.html) *Time magazine*, 9 September 1929.
[28] Geisenheyer, Max. *Mit 'Graf Zeppelin' Um Die Welt: Ein Bild-Buch*. Frankfurter Societäts-Druckerei G.m.b.H., Frankfurt am Mein (Germany), 1929.
[29] Measuring Worth - Relative Value of US Dollars. (http://www.measuringworth.com/uscompare/) (Current data is only available till 2007)
[30] Ahern, J.J. "finally sunk on November 20, 1931". (http://www.amphilsoc.org/library/exhibits/nautilus/nautilus.htm) *The Nautilus*, American Philosophical Society, 2000. Note: The scuttling was mandated by US-UK treaty.
[31] bomberguy 2008 08:15 to 09:03
[32] bomberguy 2008 07:05 to 08:14
[33] bomberguy 2008 09:30
[34] bomberguy 2008 09:50 to 10:02

LZ 127 Graf Zeppelin

[35] British Pathé News. *Graf Zeppelin crossing Atlantic* 1930- filmed onboard last stage of flight to Rio de Janeiro (http://www.youtube.com/watch?v=eyANAWnWEE4&feature=related), "Flying down to Rio" on board the giant liner of the skies, the GRAF-ZEPPELIN
[36] Post & Tele Museum Danmark. News from the Sky (http://www.postogtelemuseet.dk/zeppex/en/enSkyNews.html) Lady Drummond advertising Lucky Strike cigarettes: "I smoke a Lucky instead of eating sweets"
[37] bomberguy 2008 from 09:00 to 09:30 circles then lands
[38] Post & Tele Museum Danmark. Luftskibet Kommer (http://www.postogtelemuseet.dk/zeppex/en/enSkyOffice.html) images and movies on mail and cargo handling with the Graf
[39] Jensen, Erik. Dansk Postbefordring med Luftskib (http://www.postogtelemuseet.dk/zeppex/en/article/DanishMailPerAir.html#_ftn10)
[40] *Hindenburg's Fiery Secret* (http://shopngvideos.com/products/HindenburgsFierySecrets). [TV-Series]. National Geographic. 2000. .
[41] http://uk.youtube.com/watch?v=oVP2pZX2yGo
[42] http://www.seefunknetz.de/lzzep.htm
[43] http://www.pugetairship.org/zeppelins/list_3.html
[44] http://jadu.de/luftfahrt/zeppelin/text/bau/bau.html
[45] http://www.airships.net
[46] http://rick_oleson.tripod.com/index-53.html
[47] http://www.youtube.com/watch?v=oVP2pZX2yGo
[48] http://www.youtube.com/user/Bomberguy
[49] http://www.youtube.com/watch?v=JB6QcA2olWM
[50] http://www.youtube.com/watch?v=jO3OJdM57Js

Airship

An **airship** or **dirigible** is a lighter-than-air aircraft that can be steered and propelled through the air using rudders and propellers or other thrust. Unlike other aerodynamic aircraft such as fixed-wing aircraft and helicopters, which produce lift by moving a wing, or airfoil, through the air, aerostatic aircraft, such as airships and hot air balloons, stay aloft by filling a large cavity, such as a balloon, with a lifting gas.

The main types of airship are non-rigid (or blimps), semi-rigid and rigid. Blimps are small airships without internal skeletons. Semi-rigid airships are slightly larger and have some form of internal support such as a fixed keel. Rigid airships with full skeletons, such as the huge Zeppelin transoceanic models, all but disappeared after several high-profile catastrophic accidents during the mid-20th century.

Airships were the first aircraft to make controlled, powered flight, and were widely used before the 1940s, but their use decreased over time as their capabilities were surpassed by those of airplanes. Their decline continued with a series of high-profile accidents, including the 1937 burning of the hydrogen-filled *Hindenburg* near Lakehurst, New Jersey, and the destruction of the USS *Akron*. Airships are still used today in certain niche applications, such as advertising, tourism, camera platforms for sporting events, and aerial observation and interdiction platforms, where the ability to hover in one place for an extended period outweighs the need for speed and maneuverability.

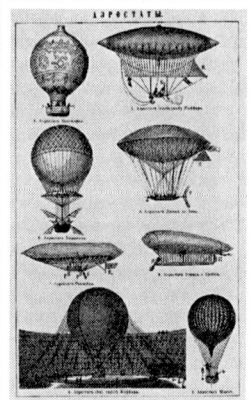

dirigible airships compared with related aerostats, from a turn of the 20th century encyclopedia

Terminology

In some countries, airships are also known as *dirigibles* from the French (*diriger* to direct plus *-ible*), meaning "directable" or steerable. The first airships were called *dirigible balloons*. Over time, the word *balloon* was dropped from the phrase. In modern usage, balloon refers to any buoyant aircraft that generally relies on wind currents for horizontal movement, and usually has a mechanism to control vertical movement.

USS *Akron* (ZRS-4) in flight on 2 November 1931

The term zeppelin is a genericised trademark that originally referred to airships manufactured by the German Zeppelin Company. The word *Luftschiff*, German for "airship", usually prefixed their crafts' names.

In modern common usage, the terms *Zeppelin*, *dirigible* and *airship* are used interchangeably for any type of rigid airship, with the term *blimp* alone used to describe non-rigid airships. Although the blimp also qualifies as a "dirigible", the term is seldom used with blimps. In modern technical usage, *airship* is the term used for all aircraft of this type, with *Zeppelin* referring only to aircraft of that manufacture, and *blimp* referring only to non-rigid airships.

There is some confusion around the term *aerostat* with regard to airships. This confusion arises because *aerostat* has two different meanings. One meaning of *aerostat* refers to all craft that remain aloft using buoyancy: here, airships are a type of *aerostat*. The narrower and more technical meaning of *aerostat* refers only to tethered or moored balloons: here, airships are distinct from *aerostats*. This airship/aerostat confusion is often exacerbated by the fact that both airships and aerostats have roughly similar shapes and comparable tail-fin configurations, although only airships have engines.

Types

- Non-rigid airships (blimps) use a pressure level in excess of the surrounding air pressure in order to retain their shape during flight.
- Semi-rigid airships, like blimps, require internal pressure to maintain their shape, but have extended, usually articulated keel frames running along the bottom of the envelope to distribute suspension loads into the envelope and allow lower envelope pressures.
- Rigid airships (Zeppelin is almost synonymous with this type) have rigid frames containing multiple, non-pressurized gas cells or balloons to provide lift. Rigid airships do not depend on internal pressure to maintain their shape and can be made to virtually any size.
- Metal-clad airships were of two kinds: rigid and non-rigid. Each kind used a thin gastight metal envelope, rather than the usual rubber-coated fabric envelope. Only four metal-clad ships are known to have been built, and only two actually flew: Schwarz's first aluminum rigid airship of 1893 collapsed,[1] while his second flew;[2] the non-rigid ZMC-2 flew 1929 to 1941;[3] while the 1929 non-rigid Slate "City of Glendale" collapsed on its first flight attempt.[4] [5] [6]

In the background, ZR-3, in front of it, (l to r) J-3 or 4, K-1, ZMC-2, in front of them, "Caquot" observation balloon, and in foreground free balloons used for training. US Navy airships and balloons, 1931

- Thermal airships use a heated lifting gas, usually air, in a fashion similar to hot air balloons.

History

Early pioneers

The father of the dirigible was Lieutenant Jean Baptiste Marie Meusnier (1754-93). On 3 December 1783, he presented a historic paper to the French Academy: "*Memoire sur l'equilbre des Machines Aerostatique*" (Memorandum on the balance of aerostatic machines). The 16 water-colour drawings published the following year depicted a 260 ft-long envelope with internal ballonnets that could be used for regulating lift, and this was attached to a long carriage that could be used as a boat if the vehicle was forced to land in water. The airship was designed to be propelled in the air by three airscrew propellers and steered with a sail-like aft rudder. In 1784, Jean-Pierre Blanchard fitted a hand-powered propeller to a balloon, the first recorded means of propulsion carried aloft. In 1785, he crossed the English Channel with a balloon equipped with flapping wings for propulsion, and a bird-like tail for steerage.[7]

Crossing of the English Channel by Blanchard in 1785.

The 19th century saw continued attempts at adding propulsion to balloons. The first aviation pioneer of Australia was Dr William Bland, a naval surgeon who was sentenced to seven years transportation in a Calcutta court after a duel in Bombay in 1813. In March 1851, Bland sent designs for his 'Atmotic Airship' to the Great Exhibition at the Crystal Palace in London where a model was displayed, this was the year before Henri Giffard flew the first steam-powered dirigible. His idea was to supply power to an elongated balloon with a steam engine installed in a car, Since the lift of the balloon was estimated at 5 tons and the car with the fuel weighed 3.5 tons, the payload was estimated at 1.5 tons. Bland believed that with two airscrews the machine could be driven at 80 km/h (50 mph) and could fly from Sydney to London in less than a week. The first person to make an engine-powered flight was Henri Giffard who, in 1852, flew 27 km (17 mi) in a steam-powered airship.[8] Airships would develop considerably over the next two decades: In 1863, Dr. Solomon Andrews devised the first fully steerable airship, the *Aereon*, although it had no motor.[9] In 1872, the French naval architect Dupuy de Lome launched a large limited navigable balloon, which was driven by a large propeller and the power of eight people.[10] It was developed during the Franco-Prussian war, as an improvement to the balloons used for communications between Paris and the countryside during the Siege of Paris by German forces, but was completed only after the end of the war.

A model of the Giffard Airship at the London Science Museum.

The navigable balloon developed by Dupuy de Lome in 1872.

Paul Haenlein flew an airship with an internal combustion engine running on the coal gas used to inflate the envelope over Vienna, the first use of such an engine to power an aircraft in 1872.[11] [12] Charles F. Ritchel made a public demonstration flight in 1878 of his hand-powered one-man rigid airship, and went on to build and sell five of his aircraft.[12]

In the 1880s a Serb named Ogneslav Kostovic Stepanovic also designed and built an airship. However, the craft was destroyed by fire before it flew. In 1883, the first electric-powered flight was made by Gaston Tissandier who fitted a 1.5 hp (1.1 kW) Siemens electric motor to an airship. The first fully controllable free-flight was made in a French

Army airship, *La France*, by Charles Renard and Arthur Constantin Krebs in 1884. The 170 ft (52 m) long, 66000 cu ft (1900 m^3) airship covered 8 km (5.0 mi) in 23 minutes with the aid of an 8.5 hp (6.3 kW) electric motor,[13] and a 435 kilograms (960 lb) battery. In 1884 and 1885, it made seven flights.[12]

In 1888, the Novelty Air Ship Company made the Air Ship for Professor Peter C. Campbell which was known as the Campbell Air Ship. The air ship was lost at sea in 1889 while being flown by Professor Hogan during an exhibition Flight. Scientific American - 27 July 1889 [14]</ref>

In 1888–97, Dr. Frederich Wölfert built three airships powered by Daimler Motor Company-built petrol engines, the last of which caught fire in flight and killed both occupants in 1897.[15] The 1888 version used a 2 hp one cylinder Daimler engine and flew 10 km from Canstatt to Kornwestheim.[16] [17]

Santos-Dumont#6 rounding the Eiffel Tower, winning the Deutsch Prize in 1901.

In 1896, a rigid airship created by Croatian engineer David Schwarz made its first flight at Tempelhof field in Berlin. After Schwarz's death, his wife, Melanie Schwarz, was paid 15,000 marks by Count → Ferdinand von Zeppelin for information about the airship.[18]

The wealthy Santos-Dumont in France had a passion for flying. Santos-Dumont designed 18 examples of balloons and dirigibles, and created 18 different examples of the latter before turning his attention to fixed winged aircraft in 1907.[19]

In 1901, Alberto Santos-Dumont, in his airship *Number 6*, a small blimp, won the Deutsch de la Meurthe prize of 100,000 francs for flying from the Parc Saint Cloud to the Eiffel Tower and back in under thirty minutes.[20] Many inventors were inspired by Santos-Dumont's small airships and a veritable airship craze began worldwide. Many airship pioneers, such as the American Thomas Scott Baldwin financed their activities through passenger flights and public demonstration flights. Others, such as Walter Wellman and Melvin Vaniman set their sights on loftier goals, attempting two polar flights in 1907 and 1909, and two trans-atlantic flights in 1910 and 1912.[21]

"The Golden Age"

The "Golden Age of Airships" began in July 1900 with the launch of the Luftschiff Zeppelin LZ1. This led to the most successful airships of all time: the Zeppelins. These were named after → Count von Zeppelin who began experimenting with rigid airship designs in the 1890s leading to the badly-flawed *LZ1* (1900) and the more successful *LZ2* (1906). At the beginning of World War I the Zeppelin airships had a framework composed of triangular lattice girders, covered with fabric and containing separate gas cells. Multi-plane, later cruciform, tail fins were used for control and stability, and two engine/crew cars hung beneath the hull driving propellers attached to the sides of the frame by means of long drive shafts. Additionally, there was a passenger compartment (later a bomb bay) located halfway between the two cars. Other airship builders were also active before the war: German firm Schütte-Lanz built the SL series from 1911; another German firm Luft-Fahrzeug-Gesellschaft built the Parseval-Luftschiff (PL) series from 1909,[22] and Italian Enrico Forlanini's firm had built and flown the first two Forlanini airships.[23]

World War I

The prospect of airships as bombers had been recognised in Europe well before the airships were up to the task. H. G. Wells' *The War in the Air* (1908) described the obliteration of entire fleets and cities by airship attack. On 5 March 1912, Italian forces became the first to use dirigibles for a military purpose during reconnaissance west of Tripoli behind Turkish lines. It was World War I, however, that marked the airship's real debut as a weapon.

Albert Caquot designed an Observation balloon for the French army in 1914. The tethered Type R Observation balloon was used by all the allied forces, including the British and United States Armies, at the end of the World War.

The Germans, French and Italians all operated airships in scouting and tactical bombing roles early in the war, and all learned that the airship was too vulnerable for operations over the front. The decision to end operations in direct support of armies was made by all in 1917.[24] [25]

Count Zeppelin and others in the German military believed they had found the ideal weapon with which to counteract British Naval superiority and strike at Britain itself. More realistic airship advocates believed the Zeppelin was a valuable long range scout/attack craft for naval operations. Raids began by the end of 1914, reached a first peak in 1915, and then were discontinued in August 1918.[26] Zeppelins proved to be terrifying but inaccurate weapons. Navigation, target selection and bomb-aiming proved to be difficult under the best of conditions. The darkness, high altitudes and clouds that were frequently encountered by Zeppelin missions reduced accuracy even further. The physical damage done by the Zeppelins over the course of the war was trivial, and the deaths that they caused (though visible) amounted to a few hundred at most. The Zeppelins were initially immune to attack by aircraft and antiaircraft guns: as the pressure in their envelopes was only just higher than ambient, holes had little effect. But once incendiary bullets were developed and used against them, their flammable hydrogen lifting gas made them vulnerable at lower altitudes. Several were shot down in flames by British defenders, and others crashed *en route*. They then started flying higher and higher above the range of other aircraft, but this made their bombing accuracy and success even worse.

Type "R" observation balloon at Arcadia Balloon School, Arcadia, Calif. 1921

In retrospect, advocates of the naval scouting role of the airship proved to be correct, and the land bombing campaign proved to be disastrous in terms of morale, men and material. Many pioneers of the German airship service died in what was the first strategic bombing campaign in history.

Countermeasures by the British were sound detection, equipment, search lights and anti-aircraft artillery, followed by night fighters in 1915. One method used early in the war when short range meant the airships had to fly from forward bases, and when only Zeppelin production facilities were in Friedrichshafen, was bombing of airship sheds by the British Royal Naval Air Service. Late in the war, the development of the aircraft carrier led to the first successful carrier air strike in history. The morning of 19 July 1918, seven Sopwith 2F.1 Camels were launched from HMS *Furious* and struck the airship base at Tondern, destroying the Zeppelins *L 54* and *L 60*.[27]

View from a French dirigible approaching a ship in 1918.

Before the World War, the British Army was interested in blimps for scouting purposes.[28] The Royal Navy, recognizing the potential threat that scouting Zeppelins might pose, decided in 1908 to produce an example of rigid airship so that the threat might be evaluated in practice instead of theory.[29] The Royal Navy was to continue development of rigid airships until the end of the war. The British Army abandoned airship development in favour of aeroplanes by the start of the war, but the Royal Navy had recognised the need for small airships to counteract the submarine and mine threat in coastal waters.[30] Beginning in February 1915, they began to deploy the SS (Sea Scout) class of blimp. These had a small envelope of 1,699-1,982 m³ (60–70,000 ft³) and at first used standard single engined planes (BE2c, Maurice Farman, Armstrong FK) shorn of wing and tail surfaces as control cars, as an economy measure. Eventually more advanced blimps with purpose built cars, such as the C (Coastal), C* (Coastal Star), NS (North Sea), SSP (Sea Scout Pusher), SSZ (Sea Scout Zero), SSE (Sea Scout Experimental) and SST (Sea Scout Twin) classes were developed. The NS class, after initial teething problems, proved to be the largest and finest airships in British service. They had a gas capacity of 360000 cu ft (10000 m³), a crew of 10 and an endurance of 24 hours. Six 230 lb (100 kg) bombs were carried, as well as three to five machine guns.

British blimps were used for scouting, mine clearance, and submarine attack duties. During the war, the British operated 226 airships, mostly non-rigid, most of which were of indigenous construction, though some non-rigid airships operated were purchased from France and even Germany (before the war).[31] Of that number several were sold to Russia, France, the US and Italy. Britain, in turn, purchased one M-type semi-rigid from Italy whose delivery was delayed until 1918. Nine rigid airships had been completed by the armistice, although several more were in an advanced state of completion by the war's end. The large number of trained crews, low attrition rate and constant experimentation in handling techniques meant that at the war's end Britain was the world leader in non-rigid airship technology.

Both France and Italy continued airships throughout the war. France preferred non-rigid types while Italy operated 49 semi-rigid airships in both the scouting and bombing roles.[32]

Airplanes had essentially replaced airships as bombers by the end of the war, and Germany's remaining zeppelins were scuttled by their crews, scrapped or handed over to the Allied powers as spoils of war. The British rigid airship program, meanwhile, had been largely a reaction to the potential threat of the German one and was largely, though not entirely, based on imitations of the German ships.

Inter-war period

A number of nations operated airships between the two world wars. Many operated blimps. Britain, the United States and Germany were the main operators of rigid airships with Italy and France using them to a lesser extent. Italy, the Soviet Union, United States and Japan mainly concentrated on semi-rigid airships.

The British *R33* and *R34* were near-identical copies of the German *L 33*, which crashed virtually intact in Yorkshire on 24 September 1916.[33] Despite being almost three years out of date by the time they were launched in 1919, they were two of the most successful in British service. The creation of the Royal Air Force (RAF) in early 1918 created a hybrid British airship program. The RAF was uninterested in airships and the Admiralty was, so a deal was made where the Admiralty would design any future military airships while the RAF would handle manpower, facilities and operations.[34]

Rescuers scramble across the wreckage of British R-38/USN ZR-2, 24 August 1921

After the armistice, the airship program was rapidly wound down, and rigid airship operations were curtailed. On 2 July 1919, *R34* began the first double crossing of the Atlantic by an aircraft. It landed at Mineola, Long Island on 6 July after 108 hours in the air. The return crossing began on 8 July because of concerns about mooring the ship in the open, and took 75 hours. Impressed, British leaders began to contemplate a fleet of airships to link Britain to its far-flung colonies. But post-war economic conditions led to the scrapping of most airships and dispersion of trained personnel, until starting construction of the *R-100* and *R-101* in 1929. The major consequence of Britain's interest in establishing airship service to the empire was the effort to use the Allies' seizure of German airships and airship sheds to avoid competition from Germany.[35] The US Navy contracted to buy the British built R-38, but before that airship was turned over to the US, it was lost to structural failure due to both improper design and operation.[36]

The first American-built rigid airship was USS *Shenandoah*, christened on 20 August in Lakehurst, New Jersey. It flew in 1923, while the *Los Angeles* was under construction. It was the first ship to be inflated with the noble gas helium, which was still so rare that the *Shenandoah* contained most of the world's reserves. When the *Los Angeles* was delivered, the two airships had to share the limited supply of Helium, and thus alternated operating and overhauls.[37]

Construction of USS *Shenandoah* (ZR-1), 1923

US Navy Zeppelin USS *Macon* (ZRS-5) over Moffett Field in 1933

The United States Navy purchased what became the USS *Los Angeles* and paid with "war reparations" money, owed according to the Versailles Treaty, thus saving The Zeppelin works. The success of the *Los Angeles* encouraged the US Navy to invest in its own, larger airships. The *Los Angeles* flew successfully for 8 years.

Meanwhile Germany was building the → *Graf Zeppelin* (LZ 127), the largest airship that could be built in the company's existing shed, and intended to stimulate interest in passenger airships. The *Graf Zeppelin* burned *blau gas*, similar to propane, stored in large gas bags below the hydrogen cells, as fuel. Since its density was similar to that of air, it avoided the weight change when fuel was used, and thus the need to valve hydrogen. The "Graf" was a great success and compiled an impressive safety record, flying over 1600000 km (990000 mi) (including the first circumnavigation of the globe by air) without a single passenger injury.[38]

The US Navy developed the idea of using airships as airborne aircraft carriers. There were two airships, the world's largest at the time, to test the principle—the USS *Akron* and *Macon*. Each carried four F9C Sparrowhawk fighters in its hangar, and could carry a fifth on the trapeze. The idea had mixed results. By the time the Navy started to develop a sound doctrine for using the ZRS-type airships, the last of the two built, USS *Macon*, was lost. The seaplane had become more mature, and was considered a better investment.[39]

USS *Akron* over Manhattan island circa 1932

Eventually the US Navy lost all three American-built rigid airships to accidents. USS *Shenandoah* on a poorly planned publicity flight flew into a severe thunderstorm over Noble County, Ohio on 3 September 1925. It broke into pieces, killing 14 of its crew. USS *Akron* was caught in a severe storm and flown into the surface of the sea off the shore of New Jersey on 3 April 1933. It carried no life boats and few life vests, so 73 of its crew of 76 died from drowning or hypothermia. USS *Macon* was lost after suffering a structural failure off the shore of Point Sur, California on 12 February 1935. The failure caused a loss of gas, which was made much worse when the aircraft was driven over pressure height causing it to lose too much helium to maintain flight.[40] Only 2 of its crew of 83 died in the crash thanks to the inclusion of life jackets and inflatable rafts after the *Akron* disaster.

Britain's Burney Scheme and decline in airships

In Britain during the 1920s, Sir Dennistoun Burney suggested a plan for air service throughout the Empire by airships (the Burney Scheme).[34] Following the election of Ramsay MacDonald, the Burney scheme was transformed into a government-controlled program, the Imperial Airship Scheme, which contracted for two airships, one to be developed by the Airship Guarantee Company, the other by the Royal Airship Works. The two designs were radically different. The "capitalist" ship, the *R100*, was conservative, while the "socialist" ship, the *R101*, was wildly innovative. Construction was delayed, and the airships did not fly until 1929. Neither airship was capable of the service intended, though the *R100* did complete a proving flight to Canada and back in 1930,[41] while the R101 crashed on its maiden voyage to France at great loss of life

In October 1930 there were rushed preparations to fly the *R101*, which had not been adequately tested and had serious deficiencies, on a flight to India carrying the Air Minister of the MacDonald government, Christopher Birdwell, Lord Thompson for an important Imperial conference. An air worthiness certificate was issued at the last moment. The *R101* left on the flight on 5 October but hours later crashed in France killing 48 of the 54 people aboard. Because of the bad publicity surrounding the crash, the Air Ministry grounded the competing *R100* in 1930 and sold it for scrap in 1931, ending the era of British rigid airships.[42]

By the mid-1930s only Germany still pursued the airship. The Zeppelin company continued to operate the *Graf Zeppelin* on passenger service between Frankfurt and Recife in Brazil, taking 68 hours. Even with the small *Graf Zeppelin*, the operation was almost profitable.[43] In the mid-1930s work started to build an airship designed specifically to operate a passenger service across the Atlantic.[44] The *Hindenburg* (LZ 129) completed a very successful 1936 season carrying passengers between Lakehurst, New Jersey and Germany. But 1937 started with the most spectacular and widely remembered airship accident. Approaching the mooring mast minutes before landing on 6 May 1937, the *Hindenburg* burst into flames and crashed. Of the 97 people aboard, 36 died: 13 passengers, 22 aircrew, and one American ground-crewman. The disaster happened before a large crowd, was filmed and a radio news reporter was cutting a recording of his coverage of the arrival. This was a disaster which theater goers could see and hear the next day. On that same next day, the *Graf Zeppelin* landed at the end of its flight from Brazil, ending intercontinental passenger airship travel.

The *Hindenburg* — moments after catching fire, 6 May 1937

Hindenburg's sister ship, the → *Graf Zeppelin II* (LZ 130), could not perform commercial passenger flights without helium, which the United States refused to sell. The *Graf Zeppelin* flew some test flights and conducted electronic espionage until 1939 when it was grounded due to the start of the war. The last two Zeppelins were scrapped in 1940.

Development of airships continued only in the United States, and in a small way, the Soviet Union.

Zeppelin Tower in Recife - The only one in the world preserved in its original structure. 2007 photo

World War II

While Germany determined that airships were obsolete for military purposes in the coming war and concentrated on the development of airplanes, the United States pursued a program of military airship construction even though it had not developed a clear military doctrine for airship use. At the Japanese attack on Pearl Harbor on 7 December 1941 that brought the United States into World War II, it had 10 non-rigid airships:

- 4 *K*-class: *K-2*, *K-3*, *K-4* and *K-5* designed as a patrol ships built from 1938.
- 3 *L*-class: *L-1*, *L-2* and *L-3* as small training ships, produced from 1938.
- 1 *G*-class built in 1936 for training.
- 2 *TC*-class that were older patrol ships designed for land forces, built in 1933. The US Navy acquired them from the United States Army in 1938.

Only *K*- and *TC*-class airships were suitable for combat and they were quickly pressed into service against Japanese and German submarines which were then sinking US shipping within visual range of the US coast. US Navy command, remembering the airship anti-submarine success from World War I, immediately requested new modern anti-submarine airships and on 2 January 1942 formed the ZP-12 patrol unit based in Lakehurst from the four *K* airships. The ZP-32 patrol unit was formed from two *TC* and two *L* airships a month later, based at NAS Moffett Field in Sunnyvale, California. An airship training base was created there as well. In December 1941 and the first months of 1942, the Goodyear blimp *Resolute* was operated as an anti-submarine privateer based out of Los Angeles. As the only US craft to operate under a Letter of Marque since the War of 1812, the *Resolute*, armed with a rifle and flown by its civilian crew, patrolled the seas for submarines.[45]

Control car of the Goodyear ZNPK (K-28) Puritan

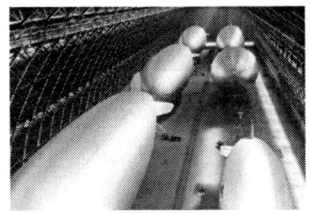

A view of six helium-filled blimps being stored in one of the two massive hangars located at NAS Santa Ana, during World War II.

In the years 1942–44, approximately 1,400 airship pilots and 3,000 support crew members were trained in the military airship crew training program and the airship military personnel grew from 430 to 12,400. The US airships were produced by the Goodyear factory in Akron, Ohio. From 1942 till 1945, 154 airships were built for the US Navy (133 *K*-class, 10 *L*-class, seven *G*-class, four *M*-class) and five *L*-class for civilian customers (serial numbers *L-4* to *L-8*).

The primary airship tasks were patrol and convoy escort near the US coastline. They also served as an organisation center for the convoys to direct ship movements, and were used in naval search and rescue operations. Rarer duties of the airships included aerophoto reconnaissance, naval mine-laying and mine-sweeping, parachute unit transport and deployment, cargo and personnel transportation. They were deemed quite successful in their duties with the highest combat readiness factor in the entire US air force (87%).

K-class blimps of USN Blimp Squadron ZP-14 conducted antisubmarine warfare operations at the Strait of Gibraltar in 1944-45.

In 1944-45, the United States Navy moved an entire squadron of eight Goodyear K class blimps (K-123, K-130, K-109, K-134, K-101, K-112, K-89, & K-114) with flight and maintenance crews from Weeksville Naval Air Station in North Carolina to Port Lyautey, French Morocco. Their mission was to locate and destroy German U-boats in the relatively shallow waters around the Strait of Gibraltar where magnetic anomaly detection (MAD) was viable. PBY aircraft had been searching these waters but MAD required low altitude flying that was dangerous at night for these aircraft. The blimps were considered a perfect solution to establish a 24/7 MAD barrier (fence) at the Straits of Gibraltar with the PBYs flying the day shift and the blimps flying the night shift. The first two blimps (K-123 & K-130) left South Weymouth NAS on 28 May 1944 and flew to Argentia, Newfoundland, the Azores, and finally to Port Lyautey where they completed the first transatlantic crossing by non-rigid airships on 1 June 1944. The blimps of USN Blimp Squadron ZP-14 (Blimpron 14, aka *The Africa Squadron*) also conducted mine-spotting and minesweeping operations in key Mediterranean ports and various escorts including the convoy carrying United States President Franklin D. Roosevelt and British Prime Minister Winston Churchill to the Yalta Conference in 1945.[46]

During the war some 532 ships without airship escort were sunk near the US coast by enemy submarines. Only one ship, the tanker *Persephone*, of the 89,000 or so in convoys escorted by blimps was sunk by the enemy.[47] Airships engaged submarines with depth charges and, less frequently, with other on-board weapons. They were excellent at driving submarines down, where their limited speed and range prevented them from attacking convoys. The weapons available to airships were so limited that until the advent of the homing torpedo they had little chance of sinking a submarine.[48]

Only one airship was ever destroyed by U-boat: on the night of 18/19 July 1943, a *K*-class airship (*K-74*) from ZP-21 division was patrolling the coastline near Florida. Using radar, the airship located a surfaced German submarine. The K-74 made her attack run but the U-boat opened fire first. *K-74*'s depth charges did not release as she crossed the U-boat and the *K-74* received serious damage, losing gas pressure and an engine but landing in the water without loss of life. The crew was rescued by patrol boats in the morning, but one crewman, Aviation Machinist's Mate Second Class Isadore Stessel, died from a shark attack. The U-Boat, *submarine U-134*, was slightly damaged and the next day or so was attacked by aircraft sustaining damage that forced it to return to base. It was finally sunk on 24 August 1943 by a British Vickers Wellington near Vigo, Spain[49] [50]

Fleet Airship Wing One operated from Lakehurst, NJ, Glynco, GA, Weeksville, NC, South Weymouth NAS Massachusetts, Brunswick NAS and Bar Harbor ME, Yarmouth, Nova Scotia, and Argentia, Newfoundland.

Some US airships saw action in the European war theatre. The ZP-14 unit operating in the Mediterranean area from June 1944 completely denied the use of the Gibraltar Straits to Axis submarines. Airships from the ZP-12 unit took part in the sinking of the last U-Boat before German capitulation, sinking *U-881* on 6 May 1945 together with destroyers Atherton and Mobery.

Other airships patrolled the Caribbean, Fleet Airship Wing Two, Headquartered at NAS Richmond, Florida, covered the Gulf of Mexico from Richmond and Key West, FL, Houma, Louisiana, as well as Hitchcock and Brownsville, Texas. FAW 2 also patrolled the northern Caribbean from San Julian, the Isle of Pines and Guantanamo Bay, Cuba as well as Vernam Field, Jamaica.

Navy blimps of Fleet Airship Wing Five, (ZP-51) operated from bases in Trinidad, British Guiana and Parmaribo, Dutch Guiana. Fleet Airship Wing Four operated along the coast of Brazil. Two squadrons, VP-41 and VP-42 flew from bases at Amapá, Igarape Assu, Sao Luiz, Fortaleza, Fernando de Noronha, Recife, Maceió, Ipitanga (near Salvador, Bahia), Caravellas, Vitoria and the hangar built for the *Graf Zeppelin* at Santa Cruz, Rio de Janeiro.

Fleet Airship Wing Three operated squadrons, ZP-32 from Moffett Field, ZP-31 at NAS Santa Ana, and ZP-33 at NAS Tillamook, Oregon. Auxiliary fields were at Del Mar, Lompoc, Watsonville and Eureka, CA, North Bend and Astoria, Oregon, as well as Shelton and Quillayute in Washington.

From 2 January 1942 till the end of war airship operations in the Atlantic, the airships of the Atlantic fleet made 37,554 flights and flew 378,237 hours. Of the over 70,000 ships in convoys protected by blimps, only one was sunk by a submarine while under blimp escort.[48]

The Soviet Union used a single airship during the war. The *W-12*, built in 1939, entered service in 1942 for paratrooper training and equipment transport. It made 1432 runs with 300 metric tons of cargo until 1945. On 1 February 1945, the Soviets constructed a second airship, a *Pobieda*-class (*Victory*-class) unit (used for mine-sweeping and wreckage clearing in the Black Sea) which crashed on 21 January 1947. Another *W*-class - W-12bis *Patriot* - was commissioned in 1947 and was mostly used for crew training, parades and propaganda.

Modern use

Although airships are no longer used for passenger transport, they are still used for other purposes such as advertising, sightseeing, surveillance and research.

One of The Goodyear Tire and Rubber Company's blimp fleet

In the 1980s, Per Lindstrand and his team introduced the *GA-42* airship, the first airship to use fly-by-wire flight control which considerably reduced the pilot's workload.

The world's largest thermal airship (300,000 cubic feet) was constructed by the Per Lindstrand company for French botanists in 1993. The *AS-300* carried an underslung raft, which was positioned by the airship on top of tree canopies in the rain forest, allowing the botanists to carry out their treetop research without significant damage to the rainforest. When research was finished at a given location, the airship returned to pick up and relocate the raft.[51]

In the spring of 2004, Lindstrand Technologies supplied the world's first fully-functional unmanned airship to the Ministry of Defense in Spain. This airship carried a 42 kilograms (93 lb) classified payload and its surveillance mission was also classified. Four years later, this airship, which is designated *GA-22*, still flies on an almost daily basis.

In June 1987, the US Navy awarded a US$168.9 million contract to Westinghouse Electric and Airship Industries of the UK to demonstrate whether a blimp could be used as an airborne platform to detect the threat of sea-skimming missiles, such as the Exocet.[52]

The *CA-80* airship, which was launched in 2000 by Shanghai Vantage Airship Manufacture Co., Ltd., had a successful trial flight in September 2001. This model of airship was designed for the purpose of advertisement and propagation, air-photo, scientific test, tour and surveillance duties. It was certified as a grade 'A' Hi-Tech introduction program (No.20000186) in Shanghai, China. The CAAC authority granted a type design approval and certificate of airworthiness for the model CA-80 airship, which has been published in the Jane's All the World's Aircraft for five times (2003–2008).[53]

In recent years, the Zeppelin company has reentered the airship business. Their new model, designated the Zeppelin NT made its maiden flight on 18 September 1997. There are currently four NT aircraft flying, a fifth completed in March 2009 and an expanded NT-14 (14,000 cubic meters of helium, capable of carrying 19 passengers) also under construction. One was sold to a Japanese company, and was planned to be flown to Japan in the summer of 2004. But due to delays getting permission from the Russian government, the company decided to transport the airship to Japan by ship. One of the four NT craft is in South Africa carrying diamond detection equipment from De Beers, an application at which the very stable low vibration NT platform excels. Some adaptations to the design for high heat operation and desert climate were part of that project. A separate mooring mast and a very heavy truck to moor the vehicle is also part of the technology.

Blimps are used for advertising and as TV camera platforms at major sporting events. The most iconic of these are the Goodyear blimps. Goodyear operates three blimps in the United States, and the Lightship group operates up to 19 advertising blimps around the world. Airship Management Services owns and operates three Skyship 600 blimps. Two operate as advertising and security ships in the North America and the Caribbean.

Skycruise Switzerland AG owns and operates two Skyship 600 blimps. One operates regularly over Switzerland used on sightseeing tours.

The Switzerland-based Skyship 600 has also played other roles over the years. For example, it was flown over Athens during the 2004 Summer Olympics as a security measure. In November 2006, it carried advertising calling it "The Spirit of Dubai" as it began a publicity tour from London to Dubai, UAE on behalf of The Palm Islands, the world's largest man-made islands created as a residential complex.

Los Angeles-based Worldwide Aeros Corp. produces FAA Type Certified Aeros 40D Sky Dragon airships.[54]

In May 2006, the US Navy began to fly airships again after a hiatus of nearly 44 years. The program uses a single American Blimp Company A-170 non-rigid airship, with designation MZ-3A. Operations focus on crew training and research, and the platform integrator is Northrop Grumman. The program is directed by the Naval Air Systems Command and is being carried out at NAES Lakehurst, the original center of US Navy lighter-than-air operations in previous decades.

The Spirit of Dubai approaches its motorised mooring mast

In November 2006, the US Army bought an A380+ airship from American Blimp Corporation through a Systems level contract with Northrop Grumman and Booz Allen Hamilton. The airship will start flight tests in late 2007 with a primary goal of carrying 2500 lb (1100 kg) of payload to an altitude of 15000 ft (4600 m) under remote control and autonomous waypoint navigation. The program will also demonstrate carrying 1000 lb (450 kg) of payload to 20000 ft (6100 m) The platform could be used for Multi-Intelligence collections. Northrop Grumman (formerly Westinghouse) has responsibility for the overall program.

In 2008 the *CA-150* airship was launched by Vantage Airship. This is an improved modification of model *CA-120* and completed manufacturing in 2008. With larger volume and increased passenger capacity, it is the largest manned non-rigid airship in China at present.[55]

Thermal airship (manufacturer GEFA-FLUG/Germany)

Several companies, such as Cameron Balloons in Bristol, United Kingdom, build hot-air airships. These combine the structures of both hot-air balloons and small airships. The envelope is the normal 'cigar' shape, complete with tail fins, but is inflated with hot air (as in a balloon) to provide the lifting force, instead of helium. A small gondola, carrying the pilot and passengers, a small engine, and the burners to provide the hot air are suspended below the envelope, below an opening through which the burners protrude.

Hot-air airships typically cost less to buy and maintain than modern helium-based blimps, and can be quickly deflated after flights. This makes them easy to carry in trailers or trucks and inexpensive to store. They are usually very slow moving, with a typical top speed of 15–20 mph (24–32 km/h, 6.7–8.9 m/s).

They are mainly used for advertising, but at least one has been used in rainforests for wildlife observation, as they can be easily transported to remote areas.

Remote controlled (RC) airships, a type of Unmanned Aerial System (UAS), are sometimes used for commercial purposes such as advertising and aerial video and photography as well as recreational purposes. They are particularly common as an advertising mechanism at indoor stadiums. While RC airships are sometimes flown outdoors, doing so for commercial purposes is illegal in the US. In particular, Docket FAA-2006-25714 states that: "The FAA recognizes that people and companies other than modelers might be flying UAS with the mistaken understanding that they are legally operating under the authority of AC 91-57. AC 91-57 only applies to modelers, and thus specifically excludes its use by persons or companies for business purposes."[56]

Recent developments

Economically, it was surprising that even in the 1930s, Zeppelins could compete with other means of transatlantic transport. Their advantage was the ability to carry significantly more passengers than other contemporary aircraft, while providing conveniences like the luxury of ship voyages. Less importantly, the technology was potentially more energy-efficient than heavier-than-air designs. On the other hand, operating the giants was quite involved, especially in terms of personnel. Often the crew would outnumber passengers on board, and on the ground large teams were necessary to assist starting and landing. Also, to accommodate Zeppelins like *Hindenburg* (which was more than five times as long as the height of the Statue of Liberty without the pedestal), very large hangars were required at airports.

Today, with large, fast, and more cost-efficient fixed-wing aircraft, it is unknown whether huge airships can operate profitably in regular passenger transport though, as energy costs rise, attention is once again returning to these lighter than air vessels as a viable alternative. At the very least, the idea of comparatively slow, "majestic" cruising at relatively low altitudes and in comfortable atmosphere certainly has retained some appeal. There have been some niches for airships in and after World War II, such as long-duration observations, antisubmarine patrol, platforms for TV camera crews, and advertising; these, however, generally require only small and flexible craft, and have thus generally been better fitted for cheaper blimps.

Heavy lifting

It has periodically been suggested that airships could be employed for cargo transport, especially delivering extremely heavy loads to areas with poor infrastructure over great distances. This has also been called Roadless trucking.[57] Also, airships could be used for heavy lifting over short distances (eg on construction sites, ...); this is described as heavy-lift, short-haul.[58] In both cases, the airships are Heavy haulers. One recent enterprise of this sort was the *Cargolifter* project, in which a hybrid (thus not entirely Zeppelin-type) airship even larger than *Hindenburg* was projected. Around 2000, this idea was realized, when the CargoLifter AG constructed the world's largest cantilever shop hall measuring 360 m (1200 ft) long, 210 m (690 ft) wide and 107 m (350 ft) high about 60 km (37 mi) south of Berlin. In May 2002, the project was stopped for financial reasons; the company had to file bankruptcy. Although no rigid airships are currently used for heavy lifting, hybrid airships are being developed for such purposes. John McPhee's *The Deltoid Pumpkin Seed* is the story of one company attempting this.

Passenger transport

A small company in Germany is currently examining the possibility of building a cruise airship, for now known as the *Zeppelin ET* (for Euro Tour); it will be able to carry passengers on week-long cruises at comfort levels and prices comparable to those of luxury sea cruises of similar duration. However, although this airship bears the name "Zeppelin", it is not a rigid but a semi-rigid airship (even though "zeppelin" has come to be almost a synonym for rigid airship). The project is still in its early stages and nothing practical has resulted as of 2004.

In the 1990s, the successor of the original Zeppelin company in Friedrichshafen, the *Zeppelin Luftschifftechnik GmbH*, reengaged in airship construction. The first experimental craft (later christened *Friedrichshafen*) of the type *Zeppelin NT* flew in September 1997. Though larger than common blimps, the *Neue Technologie* (new technology) Zeppelins are much smaller than their giant ancestors and not actually Zeppelin-types in the classical sense; they are

A Zeppelin NT airship

sophisticated semi-rigids. Apart from the greater payload, their main advantages compared to blimps are higher speed and excellent maneuverability. Meanwhile, several *Zeppelin NT* have been produced and operated profitably in joyrides, research flights and similar applications.

In June 2004, a Zeppelin NT was sold for the first time to a Japanese company, Nippon Airship Corporation, for tourism and advertising mainly around Tokyo. It was also given a role at the 2005 Expo in Aichi. The aircraft began a flight from Friedrichshafen to Japan, stopping at Geneva, Paris, Rotterdam, Munich, Berlin, Stockholm and other European cities to carry passengers on short legs of the flight. However, Russian authorities denied overflight permission so the airship had to be dismantled and shipped to Japan rather than following the historic *Graf Zeppelin* flight from Germany to Japan.

In 2007, Airship Ventures Inc. began operations from Moffett Federal Airfield near Mountain View, California and currently offers tours of the San Francisco Bay Area for up to 12 passengers.

Use in exploration

In November 2005, De Beers, the diamond mining company, launched an airship exploration program over the remote Kalahari desert. A Zeppelin, loaded with high-tech equipment, is used to find potential diamond mines by scanning the local geography for low-density rock formations - so-called kimberlite pipes. On 21 September 2007, the airship was severely damaged by a whirlwind while in Botswana. One crew member, who was on watch aboard the moored craft, was slightly injured but released after overnight observation in hospital.

Present-day research

Prototypes and experimental models

Hybrid designs such as the Heli-Stat airship/helicopter, the Aereon aerostatic/aerodynamic craft, and the Cyclocrane (a hybrid aerostatic/rotorcraft), have struggled to take flight. The Cyclocrane was also interesting in that the airship's envelope rotated along its longitudinal axis.

CL 160 was a very large semi-rigid airship to be built by the start-up Cargolifter, but funding ran out in 2002 after a massive hangar was built. The hangar, built just outside Berlin, has since been converted into a resort called Tropical Islands.

In 2005, a short-lived project of the US Defense Advanced Research Projects Agency (DARPA) was WALRUS HULA which explored the potential for using airships as long-distance, heavy lift craft.[59] [60] The primary goal of the research program was to determine the feasibility of building an airship capable of carrying 500 short tons (450 t) of payload a distance of 12000 mi (19000 km) and land on an unimproved location without the use of external ballast or ground equipment (such as masts). In 2005, two contractors, Lockheed Martin and US Aeros Airships were each awarded approximately $3 million to do feasibility studies of designs for WALRUS. In late March 2006, DARPA announced the termination of work on WALRUS after completion of the current Phase I contracts.

The US government is funding two major projects in the high altitude arena. The Composite Hull High Altitude Powered Platform (CHHAPP) is sponsored by US Army Space and Missile Defense Command. This aircraft is also sometimes called *HiSentinel High-Altitude Airship*. This prototype ship made a five-hour test flight in September 2005. The second project, the high-altitude airship (HAA), is sponsored by DARPA. In 2005, DARPA awarded a contract for nearly $150 million to Lockheed Martin for prototype development. First flight of the HAA is planned for 2008.

Many companies are working on high-altitude airships.

In 1999 Lindstrand Technologies, in partnership with Daimler Chrysler Aerospace of Germany, was awarded a design contract by the European Space Agency (ESA) to develop a High Altitude Long Endurance airship for possible use in the telecommunications market.[61] As a result of this, Per Lindstrand was awarded the German-based Körber Prize for engineering excellence. These stratospheric long endurance platforms inhabit the calm upper atmosphere at usually 70,000 ft where airspace is uncontrolled, in a geo-synchronous position and remain in the same place by motoring into the prevailing wind. About 200 and 300 ft long, they are intended to stay up for a period of three to five years without maintenance. Applications include cellular phone (S-UMTS) base station, passenger information system, digital broadcast, remote monitoring, metropolitan area network and emergency response network.

E-Green Technologies, Inc., is developing a high-altitude version of their spherically and bullet shaped airships. JP Aerospace has discussed its long-range plans that include not only high altitude communications and sensor applications but also an "orbital airship" capable of lifting cargo into low Earth orbit with a marginal transportation cost of $1 per short ton per mile of altitude (0.70 US$/t·km).

On 31 January 2006 LockheedMartin made the first flight of their secretly built hybrid airship designated the P-791. The design is very similar to the SkyCat, unsuccessfully promoted for many years by the now financially troubled British company Advanced Technology Group. Although Lockheed Martin is developing a design for the DARPA WALRUS HULA project, it claimed that the P-791 is unrelated to WALRUS. Nonetheless, the design represents an approach that may well be applicable to WALRUS. Some believe that Lockheed Martin had used the secret P-791 program as a way to get a "head start" on the other WALRUS competitor, US Aeros Airships.

A privately funded effort to build a heavy-lift aerostatic/aerodynamic hybrid craft, called the Dynalifter, is being carried out by Ohio Airships [62]. Test flights are to begin in Spring 2006.

The research and development company for airship technologies, 21st century Airships Inc., has developed a spherical-shaped airship, and airships for high altitude, environmental research, surveillance and military applications, heavy lift and sightseeing. Its airships have set numerous world records.

In Russia, AUGUR-RosAerosystems Group is manufacturing non-rigid multi-functional airships for up to ten passengers, as well as patrol airships including the Au-12 and Au-30. They are also working on developmental programs for heavy-lift cargo models and high-altitude stratospheric ships.

Airships in Planetary Exploration

Several proposals have been made for the use of airships in the robotic exploration of those planets (and one moon, Titan) which have atmosphere thick enough to provide buoyancy. Some of these applications are discussed under Aerobots.

Proposed designs and applications

Heavy lifting

The proposed Aeroscraft is Aeros Corporation's continuation of the now canceled WALRUS project. The Aeroscraft is not an airship or hybrid airship; it is a new type of buoyancy assisted air vehicle. Unlike any other aircraft the Aeroscraft generates lift through a combination of aerodynamics, thrust vectoring and gas buoyancy generation and management, and for much of the time will fly heavier than air.

Passenger transport

There is a case for the airship or zeppelin as a medium to long distance air 'cruise ship' using helium as a lifting agent. Airship passengers could have spacious decks inside the hull to give ample room for sitting, sleeping and recreation. There would be ample room for restaurants and similar facilities. The potential exists for a market in more leisurely journeys, such as cruises over scenic terrain.

Undeveloped ideas

- Vacuum airship A theoretical design for an airship using the absence of something for lift proposed by Francisco De Lana, a Jesuit monk.
- Hybrid airship is a general term for an aircraft that combines characteristics of heavier-than-air (airplane or helicopter) and lighter-than-air technology. Examples include helicopter/airship hybrids intended for heavy lift

applications and dynamic lift airships intended for long-range cruising. It should be noted that most airships, when fully loaded with cargo and fuel, are usually ballasted to be heavier than air, and thus must use their propulsion system and shape to create aerodynamic lift, necessary to stay aloft; technically making them hybrid airships. However, the term 'hybrid airship' refers to craft that obtain a significant portion of their lift from aerodynamic lift and often require substantial take-off rolls before becoming airborne.

Practical comparison with heavier-than-air aircraft

The advantage of airships over airplanes is that static lift sufficient for flight is generated by the lifting gas and requires no engine power. This was an immense advantage before the middle of World War I and remained an advantage for long distance, or long duration operations until World War II. Modern concepts for high altitude airships include photovoltaic cells to reduce the need to land to refuel, thus they can remain in the air until consumables expire.

The disadvantages are that an airship has a very large reference area and comparatively large drag coefficient, thus a larger drag force compared to that of airplanes and even helicopters. Given the large flat plate area and wetted surface of an airship, a practical limit is reached around 80–100 miles per hour (130–160 km/h). Thus airships are used where speed is not critical.

The altitude an airship can fly at largely depends on how much lifting gas it can lose due to expansion before stasis is reached. The ultimate altitude record for a rigid airship was set in 1917 by the L-55 under the command of Hans-Kurt Flemming when he forced the airship to 24000 ft (7300 m) attempting to cross France after the "Silent Raid" on London. The L-55 lost lift as the descent to lower altitudes over Germany compressed the gas left in the cells, and thus the weight of air displaced. L-55 crashed due to loss of lift.[63] While such waste of gas was necessary for the survival of airships in the later years of WW I, it was impractical for commercial operations, or operations of helium-filled military airships. The highest flight made by a hydrogen filled passenger airship was 5500 ft (1700 m) on the *Graf Zeppelin's* around the world flight.[64] The practical limit for rigid airships was about 3000 feet (900 m), and for pressure airships around 8000 ft (2400 m).

Modern airships use dynamic helium volume. At sea level altitude, helium only takes up a small part of the hull, while the rest is filled with air. As the airship ascends, the helium inflates with reduced outer pressure, and air is pushed out and released from the downward valve. This allows an airship to reach any altitude with balanced inner and outer pressure if the buoyancy is enough. Some civil aerostats could reach 100000 ft (30000 m) without explosion due to overloaded inner pressure.

The greatest disadvantage of the airship is size, which is essential to increasing performance. As size increases, the problems of ground handling increase geometrically.[65] As the German Navy transitioned from the "p" class Zeppelins of 1915 with a volume of over 1100000 cu ft (31000 m^3) to the larger "q" class of 1916, the "r" class of 1917, and finally the "w" class of 1918, at almost 2200000 cu ft (62000 m^3) ground handling problems reduced the number of days the Zeppelins were able to make patrol flights. This availability declined from 34% in 1915, to 24.3% in 1916 and finally 17.5% in 1918.[66]

So long as the power-to-weight ratios of aircraft engines remained low and specific fuel consumption high, the airship had an edge for long range or duration operations. As those figures changed, the balance shifted rapidly in the airplane's favor. By mid-1917 the airship could no longer survive in a combat situation where the threat was airplanes. By the late 1930s, the airship barely had an advantage over the airplane on intercontinental over-water flights, and that advantage had vanished by the end of WW II.

This is in face-to-face tactical situation, current High Altitude Airship project is planned to survey hundreds of kilometers as their operation radius, often much farther than normal engage range of a military airplane. This provides better early warning, even farther than the Aegis system. The current Aegis system is often based on a sea vessel like Ticonderoga Class and Burke Class, which have restricted radio horizon and line of sight. For example, a radar mounted on a vessel platform 30 m (100 ft) high has radio horizon at 20 km (12 mi) range, while a radar at

18000 m (59000 ft) altitude has radio horizon at 480 km (300 mi) range. This is significantly important for detecting low-flying cruise missiles or fighter-bombers.

The blimp remained a viable military system only until the conventional submarine was replaced by the nuclear submarine. Today, airships are used primarily for command, control and as a communication platform; to establish and maintain reliable and secure connectivity among all forces, provide transparent data across the echelons; precisely locate friendly and enemy forces; detect targets on an extended battlefield at a minimal exposure to enemy forces; real time targeting; navigation assistance; battle management; monitor radio conversations, etc.

Safety

The most commonly used lift gas, helium, is not merely inert but acts as a fire extinguisher, since it is non-flammable.[67] Furthermore, one of the main factors of the Hindenburg's destruction lay beyond its hydrogen contents: the materials that made up its skin were flammable. Modern designs can use much less flammable materials. Modern airships have a natural buoyancy and special design that offers a virtually zero catastrophic failure mode. While on long-haul flights weather patterns would be flown to avoid bad weather, the hull's mass largely dampens the effect of turbulence, just as a large tanker rides through rough seas. An airship is usually a poor lightning target, as it is constructed mainly from composite materials. If it is struck, built-in protection devices minimise the risk to the vehicle and its cargo.

A series of structural vulnerability tests were done by the UK Defence Evaluation and Research Agency DERA on a Skyship 600, an earlier airship built by the Munk team to a similar pressure-stabilised design. Several hundred high-velocity bullets were fired through the hull, and even two hours later the vehicle would have been able to return to base. The airship is virtually impervious to automatic rifle and mortar fire: ordnance passes through the envelope without causing critical helium loss. In all instances of light armament fire evaluated under both test and live conditions, the vehicle was able to complete its mission and return to base. The internal hull pressure is maintained at only 1–2% above surrounding air pressure, the vehicle is highly tolerant to physical damage or to attack by small-arms fire or missiles.[68]

See also

- Airships by country
- Evolutionary Air and Space Global Laser Engagement
- High Altitude Platforms
- Hyperion airship, fictional airship type.
- List of airship accidents
- → List of Zeppelins
- Mystery airship
- Stratellite
- SVAM CA-80
- Vertical airship

Bibliography

- Althoff, William F., *USS Los Angeles: The Navy's Venerable Airship and Aviation Technology*, 2003, ISBN 1-57488-620-7
- Archbold, Rich and Ken Marshall, *Hindenburg, an Illustrated History*, 1994 ISBN 0-446-51784-4
- Botting, Douglas, *Dr. Eckener's Dream Machine*. New York Henry Hold and Company, 2001, ISBN 0-8050-6458-3
- Brooks, Peter, W., *Zeppelin: Rigid Airships 1893–1940*, Washington, Smithsonian Institution Press, 1992, ISBN 1-56098-228-4
- Brooks, Peter, *Zeppelin: Rigid Airships 1893–1940*, 2004, ISBN 0-85177-845-3
- Burgess, Charles P., *Airship Design*, (1927) 2004 ISBN 1-4102-1173-8
- Cross, Wilbur, *Disaster at the Pole*, 2002 ISBN 1-58574-496-4
- Dick, Harold G., with Robinson, Douglas H., *Graf Zeppelin & Hindenburg*, Washington, D.C., Smithsonian Institution Press, 1985, ISBN
- Dooley, Sean C., The Development of Material-Adapted Structural Form [69] - Part II: Appendices [70]. THÈSE NO 2986 (2004), École Polytechnique Fédérale de Lausanne
- Frederick, Arthur, et al., *Airship saga: The history of airships seen through the eyes of the men who designed, built, and flew them*, 1982, ISBN 0-7137-1001-2
- Griehl, Manfred and Joachim Dressel, *Zeppelin! The German Airship Story*, 1990, ISBN 1-85409-045-3
- Higham, Robin, *The British Rigid Airship, 1908–1931: A study in weapons policy*, London, G. T. Foulis, 1961, OCLC 830820 [71]
- Khoury, Gabriel Alexander (Editor), *Airship Technology (Cambridge Aerospace Series)*, 2004, ISBN 0-521-60753-1
- Leasor, James, *The Millionth Chance*, New York, Reynal and Company, 1957, LCC 58-7405
- Ligugnana, Sandro THE HISTORY - Enrico Formanini and the Officine Leonardo da Vinci [72], LPVC S.p.A. retrieved on 30 June 2008
- Lueger, Otto: Lexikon der gesamten Technik und ihrer Hilfswissenschaften, Bd. 1 Stuttgart, Leipzig 1920. digital scan [73] **(German)**
- McKee, Alexander, *Ice crash*, 1980, ISBN 0-312-40382-8
- Meiklejohn, Bernard (December 1906). "The Conquest of the Air [74]". *The World's Work: A History of Our Time* **XIII**: 8283-8210.
- Morgala, Andrzej, *Sterowce w II Wojnie Światowej* (Airships in the Second World War), Lotnictwo, 1992 **(Polish)**
- Mowthorpe, Ces, *Battlebags: British Airships of the First World War*, 1995 ISBN 0-905778-13-8
- Robinson, Douglas H., *Giants in the Sky*, University of Washington Press, 1973, ISBN 0-295-95249-0
- Robinson, Douglas H., *The Zeppelin in Combat: A history of the German Naval Airship Division, 1912-1918*, Atglen, PA, Shiffer Publications, 1994, ISBN 0-88740-510-X
- Smith, Richard K. *The Airships Akron & Macon: flying aircraft carriers of the United States Navy*, Annapolis MD, US Naval Institute Press, 1965, ISBN 978-0-87021-065-5
- Shock, James R., Smith, David R., *The Goodyear Airships*, Bloomington, Illinois, Airship International Press, 2002, ISBN 0-9711637-0-7
- Squier, George Owen (1908). "The Present Status of Military Aeronautics [75]". *Annual Report of The Board Of Regents Of The Smithsonian Institution*: 143-144. Retrieved 7 August 2009.
- Toland, John, *Ships in the Sky*, New York, Henry Hold; London, Muller, 1957, OCLC 2905721 [76]
- Vaeth, J. Gordon, *Blimps & U-Boats*, Anapolis, Maryland, US Naval Institute Press, 1992, ISBN 1-55750-876-3
- Ventry, Lord; Kolesnik, Eugene, *Jane's Pocket Book 7: Airship Development*, 1976 ISBN 0-356-04656-7
- Ventry, Lord; Koesnik, Eugene M., *Airship Saga*, Poole, Dorset, Blandford Press, 1982, p. 97 ISBN 0-7137-1001-2

- Winter, Lumen; Degner, Glenn, *Minute Epics of Flight*, New York, Grosset & Dunlap, 1933. OCLC 738688 [77]
- US War Department, *Airship Aerodynamics: Technical Manual*, (1941) 2003, ISBN 1-4102-0614-9

External links

- Airships.net: Illustrated history of airships [78]
- **(French)** Le Hangar à dirigeables d'Ecauseville [79]
- Airships [80] at the Open Directory Project
- US Navy Airship History [81]
- Ferdinand von Zeppelin, US PAT No. 621,195 [82], *Navigable Balloon*. 14 March 1899.
- Historic Farnborough - home to early balloon development including the Nulli Secundus [83]
- The Imperial (British) Airship Programme 1924-30 [84]
- A new age for Dirigibles [85], *New York Times* slide show, 6 July 2008
- Dirigibles of Imperial Russia (up to 1917 year) [86], 28 February 2008, info.dolgopa.org
- an airship caught on Google Street View [87] over London's Elephant & Castle around the time the Spirit of Dubai's tour was launched

References

[1] Dooley, A.185-A.186 citing Robinson, pp.2-3 collapsed on inflation
[2] Dooley, A.193 (at Tempelhof, Berlin in 1897, landed but then collapsed)
[3] NAS Grosse Ile (http://nasgi.org/zmc2.htm), NASGIVM. 2006.
[4] National Air and Space Museum, Smithsonian Institution. 2008. Slate Aircraft Corporation City of Glendale Negatives, Accession number 2006-0039 (http://siris-archives.si.edu/ipac20/ipac.jsp?uri=full=3100001~!270817!0)
[5] City of Glendale. Photo Album (http://www.ci.glendale.ca.us/GCATG/pages/photo_album/1920s_3.htm). Retrieved 3 September 2008.
[6] Both non-rigid ships nevertheless had strong metal monocoque envelopes which, while they maintained their shape uninflated, required an overpressure during flight.
[7] Winter & Degner (1933), pp. 26–27.
[8] Winter & Degner (1933), p. 36.
[9] Toland (1957), pp. 13–24.
[10] Brooks 1992 p. 19.
[11] Winter & Degner (1933), p. 44.
[12] Bento S. Mattos, Short History of Brazilian Aeronautics (http://pdf.aiaa.org/preview/CDReadyMASM06_778/PV2006_328.pdf) (PDF), 44th AIAA Aerospace Sciences Meeting and Exhibit, Reno, Nevada, 9-12 January 2006.
[13] Winter & Degner (1933), pp. 49–50.
[14] http://www.scripophily.net/noairshco.html
[15] Brooks 1992 p. 20.
[16] Mercedes-Benz Museum (Trip II): The beginning (http://www.gminsidenews.com/forums/f62/mercedes-benz-museum-trip-ii-beginning-52297/), *gminsidenews.com*, 2007.
[17] Member's Circular Letter February 2008, (http://www.zeppelin-tourismus.de/en/rund0208e.pdf) *zeppelin-tourismus.de*.
[18] Brooks 1992 pp. 27–31.
[19] Niccoli, R. *The Book of Flight: From the flying machines of Leonardo da Vinci to the conquest of space*, New York, Friedman/Fairfax, 2002, p. 24. ISBN 978-1-58663-716-3
[20] Toland (1957), pp. 25–37.
[21] Toland (1957), pp. 49–51.
[22] Lueger 1920, pp.404-412, Luftschiff (http://www.zeno.org/Lueger-1904/A/Luftschiff)
[23] Ligugnana, Sandro
[24] Ventry & Koesnik (1982), p. 85.
[25] Robinson (1973), pp. 126–127.
[26] Robinson (1994), p. 360.
[27] Robinson (1994), pp. 340–341.
[28] Higham (1961), p. 25.
[29] Higham (1961), p. 40.
[30] Higham (1961), p. 111.
[31] Mowthorpe, Ces, *Battlebags*, Stroud, Gloucs, Allan Sutton Publishing, 1995, p. xxiii.

[32] Ventry & Koesnik (1982), p. 97.
[33] Higham (1961), p. 138.
[34] Higham (1961), p. 176.
[35] Higham (1961), p. 191.
[36] Higham (1961), pp. 222–223.
[37] Althoff, William F., *USS Los Angeles*, Washington DC, Brassey's, 2004, p. 48, ISBN 1-57488-620-7
[38] Botting, Douglas, *Dr. Eckener's Dream Machine*, New York, Henry Hold, 2001, ISBN 0-8050-6458-3
[39] Smith (1965), pp. 171–174.
[40] Smith (1965), pp. 157–161.
[41] Countryman, Barry, *R100 in Canada*, Erin, Ontario, Boston Mills, 1982, ISBN 0-919822-36-3
[42] Leasor, James, *The Millionth Chance*, New York, Reynal, 1957, LCC 58-7405
[43] Botting, Douglas, *Dr. Eckener's Dream Machine*. New York, Henry Hold, 2001, p. 235, ISBN 0-8050-6458-3
[44] Dick, Harold G., with Robinson, Douglas H., *Graf Zeppelin & Hindenburg*, Washington DC, Smithsonian Institution Press, 1985, p. 83, ISBN 0-87474-346-8
[45] Shock, James R.; Smith, David R., *The Goodyear Airships*, Bloomington IL, Airship International Press, 2002, p. 43, ISBN 0-9711637-0-7
[46] Kaiser, Don, Blimp Squadron 14 (http://www.warwingsart.com/LTA/zp-14.html), *WarWingsArt.com*, retrieved 16 September 2009.
[47] Vaeth, J. Gordon, *Blimps & U-Boats*, Anapolis, MD, US Naval Institute Press, 1992, pp. 20–21, ISBN 1-55750-876-3
[48] Vaeth, J. Gordon, *Blimps & U-Boats*, Anapolis, MD, US Naval Institute Press, 1992, ISBN 1-55750-876-3
[49] U.S. Navy LTA history (http://www.history.navy.mil/download/lta-08.pdf).
[50] U-134 history (http://uboat.net/boats/u134.htm), *Uboat.net*.
[51] *Thermal Airships* (http://www.lindstrandtech.com/thermal_airships.html), Lindstrand Technologies.
[52] Reuters, "Navy Awards Blimp Order" (http://query.nytimes.com/gst/fullpage.html?res=9B0DEFDC1E30F935A35755C0A961948260), *New York Times*, 6 June 1987.
[53] CA-80 Blimp from 2000 (http://www.vantageship.com/en_ca80data.htm)
[54] Worldwide Aeros Corp. website (http://www.aerosml.com).
[55] CA-150 Blimp from 2008 (http://www.vantageship.com/en_zairenfeiting.htm)
[56] FAA Docket FAA-2006-25714 (http://www.faa.gov/aircraft/air_cert/design_approvals/uas/reg/media/frnotice_uas.pdf), Federal Aviation Authority.
[57] "Roadless trucking" (http://www.dynalifter.com/Dynaliftercom/RoadlessTrucking.htm), Dynalifter.
[58] "Boeing and SkyHook International to Build JHL-40 Heavy-Lift Rotorcraft" (http://www.deagel.com/news/Boeing-and-SkyHook-International-to-Build-JHL-40-Heavy-Lift-Rotorcraft_n000004518.aspx), press release, 8 July 2008.
[59] "Contractors for Walrus Program announced" (http://www.darpa.mil/news/2005/walrus.pdf), press release, Defense Advanced Research Projects Agency, 26 August 2005.
[60] "US CBO Gives OK to HULA Airships for Airlift" (http://www.defenseindustrydaily.com/2005/10/us-cbo-gives-ok-to-hula-airships-for-airlift/index.php), *Defense Industry Daily*, 21 October 2005.
[61] High Altitude Long Endurance Airships (http://www.lindstrandtech.com/hale.html), Lindstrand Technologies.
[62] http://www.ohio-airships.com/
[63] Robinson (1994), p. 294.
[64] "Honors to Dr. Hugo Eckener: The First Airship Flight Around the World", *National Geographic*, Vol. LVII, No. 6, June 1930, p. 679.
[65] Brooks 1992 pp. 7-8
[66] Robinson (1994), p. 373.
[67] Stwertka, Albert, *Guide to the Elements: Revised Edition*. New York; Oxford University Press, 1998, p. 24. ISBN 0-19-512708-0
[68] High Safety Level (page 5) and Structural Vulnerability Tests (page 7) (http://www.worldskycat.com/images/SkyCat.pdf). World Skycat. Retrieved 25 April 2008.
[69] http://biblion.epfl.ch/EPFL/theses/2004/2986/EPFL_TH2986_screen.pdf
[70] http://biblion.epfl.ch/EPFL/theses/2004/2986/EPFL_TH2986_app_screen.pdf
[71] http://www.worldcat.org/oclc/830820
[72] http://www.officineleonardo.com/storia/uk/0001.html
[73] http://www.zeno.org/Lueger-1904
[74] http://books.google.com/books?id=3IfNAAAAMAAJ&pg=PA8283
[75] http://books.google.com/books?id=gtQWAAAAYAAJ&pg=PA117
[76] http://www.worldcat.org/oclc/2905721
[77] http://www.worldcat.org/oclc/738688
[78] http://www.airships.net/
[79] http://www.aerobase.fr/
[80] http://www.dmoz.org/Recreation/Aviation/Aircraft/Airships/
[81] http://www.history.navy.mil/branches/lta-m.html
[82] http://www.google.com/patents?vid=621195
[83] http://www.historicfarnborough.co.uk/

[84] http://www.airshipsonline.com/airships/imperial/index.html
[85] http://www.nytimes.com/slideshow/2008/07/06/business/0706-BLIMP_index.html
[86] http://info.dolgopa.org/album/06_00e.htm
[87] http://maps.google.co.uk/?ie=UTF8&layer=c&cbll=51.494747,-0.097507&panoid=eSaZwLUG51hqyY4RnXdozQ&cbp=12,103.
8267237267845,,3,-15.980747767857144&ll=51.494717,-0.097353&spn=0,359.990387&z=17

Ferdinand von Zeppelin

Ferdinand Adolf Heinrich August Graf von Zeppelin[1] (also known as Ferdinand Graf von Zeppelin[2] [3], Graf Zeppelin and in English, **Count Zeppelin**) (8 July 1838 – 8 March 1917) was a German general and later aircraft manufacturer, the founder of the Zeppelin → Airship company. He was born in Konstanz, Grand Duchy of Baden (now part of Baden-Württemberg, Germany).

Ferdinand von Zeppelin.

Family and personal life

Isabella Gräfin von Zeppelin

Ferdinand was the son of Württemberg Minister and Hofmarschall Friedrich Jerôme Wilhelm Karl Graf von Zeppelin (1807–1886) and his wife Amélie Françoise Pauline (born Macaire d'Hogguer) (1816–1852). Ferdinand spent his childhood with his sister and brother at their Girsberg manor near Constance, where he was educated by private resident teachers.[4] and lived there until his death.[5]

In Berlin on 7 August 1869 Ferdinand married Isabella Freiin von Wolff from the house of Alt-Schwanenburg (Livonia).[6] They had a daughter, Helene (Hella) von Zeppelin (1879–1967) who in 1909 married Alexander Graf von Brandenstein-Zeppelin (1881–1949).

Ferdinand had a nephew Baron Max von Gemmingen who was to later volunteer at the start of World War I, after he was past military age, to become general staff officer assigned to the military airship LZ 12 Sachsen.[7]

Army career

In 1853 Count Zeppelin left to attend the polytechnic at Stuttgart, and in 1855 he became a cadet of the military school at Ludwigsburg and then started his career as an army officer in the army of Württemberg.[4]

By 1858 Zeppelin was Leutnant in the Army of Württemberg and that year he was given leave to study science, engineering and chemistry at Tübingen. The Prussians mobilising for the Austro-Sardinian War interrupted this study in 1859 when he was called up to the *Ingenieurkorps* (Prussian engineering corps) at Ulm.[8]

In 1863 Zeppelin took leave to act as an observer for the Northern Potomac army in the American Civil War against the Confederates, and later took part in an expedition with Russians and Indians to the source of the Mississippi river and he made his first ascent with Steiner's captive balloon.

appointed adjutant in 1865

In 1865 Zeppelin is appointed adjutant of the King of Württemberg and as general staff officer participates in the Austro-Prussian War of 1866 and is awarded the Ritterkreuz (Knight's Cross) of the Order of Distinguished Service of Württemberg.[4] In the Franco-Prussian War of 1870/1871 his extended ride behind enemy lines (an example of reconnaissance in force) made him famous among Germans.

From 1882 until 1885 Zeppelin was commander of the Uhlan regiment in Ulm, and lastly as envoy of Württemberg in Berlin.

In 1890 his role as commander was criticised,[9] leading to his fall from imperial grace and he had to retire from the Army, albeit with the rank of Generalleutnant.[5]

Zeppelin in 1900

Airships

Ferdinand von Zeppelin visited the balloon camp of Prof. Thaddeus S. C. Lowe during the Peninsular Campaign of the American Civil War. The balloons were placed off limits to civilian riders and Lowe was not to entertain the curious von Zeppelin. He sent him to another balloon camp where the German aeronaut John Steiner could be of more help to the young man. In 1869 von Zeppelin returned to America to meet and learn from the experienced Prof. Lowe to gain all the knowledge he could in ballooning.

From the 1880s onward, Zeppelin was preoccupied with the idea of guidable balloons. He had already outlined an overall construction system in 1874,[10] and had written to the King of Württemberg stating that Germany was behind France and that only large airships were practical for military use.[11]

After his forced resignation from the military in 1890, Zeppelin worked fulltime on his concept. He hired engineer Theodor Gross to make tests of possible materials, and had the engines of the time assessed for both fuel efficiency and power to weight ratio. He also had air propellers tested and strove to obtain higher purity hydrogen gas from suppliers.[12] Zeppelin was so confident of his concept that in June 1891 he wrote to the King of Württemberg's secretary, announcing he was to start building, and shortly after requested a review from the Prussian Army's Chief of General Staff. The next day Zeppelin gave up as he realised he had underestimated air resistance such that the best engines of the time would not achieve a sufficient velocity.[13]

Zeppelin rethought his position and resumed work on hearing that Rudolf Hans Bartsch von Sigsfeld made light but powerful engines, information soon shown to be overoptimistic. Whereupon Zeppelin urged his supporter Max von Duttenhofer to press Daimler-Motoren-Gesellschaft for more efficient engines so as not to fall behind the French.[14] Duttenhofer wrote to Gross threatening to withdraw support, and Zeppelin shortly sacked Gross, citing Gross' lack of support and that he was "an obstacle in my path".[14]

Despite these setbacks Zeppelin's organization had refined his idea: a rigid aluminium framework covered in a fabric envelope; separate multiple internal gas cells, each free to expand and contract thus obviating the need for ballonets; modular frame allowing addition of sections and gas cells; controls, engines and gondola rigidly attached. After publishing the idea in 1892 he hired engineer Theodor Kober who started work testing and further refining the design.[15] Zeppelin submitted Kober's 1893 detailed designs to the Prussian Airship Service,[16] whose committee reviewed it in 1894.[16] In June 1895 this committee then recommended minimum funds be granted, but withdrew and finally rejected the design in July.[17]

On month later, in August 1895, Zeppelin received a patent for Kober's design, described as an "airship-train" (*Lenkbarer Luftfahrzug mit mehreren hintereinanderen angeordneten Tragkörpern.*)[18] [19]

In early 1896 Zeppelin's lecture on steerable airship designs given to the Association of German Engineers (VDI) so impressed them that the VDI launched a public appeal for financial support for him.[19] This led to a first contact with Carl Berg who supplied aluminium alloys which Zeppelin had tested, and by May 1898 they, together with Philipp Holzmann,[20] Daimler, Max von Eyth, Carl von Linde, and Friedrich Voith, had formed the joint stock company *Gesellschaft zur Förderung der Luftschiffart*.[19] Zeppelin invested 441,000 Marks, over half the total capital.[19] [20] Actual construction then started of what was to be the first successful rigid airship, the Zeppelin LZ1. Legends later arose that Zeppelin had used the patent and design of David Schwarz's airship of 1897,[21] [22] but these were rejected by Eckener in 1938[22] and by later reviewers. Zeppelin's design was "radically different"[23] in both its scale and its framework from that of Schwarz.

Zeppelin made three flights with the LZ 1 over the Bodensee. The flights became more and more successful, igniting a public euphoria which allowed the Count to pursue the development of his vehicle. In fact, the second version of his airship was entirely financed through donations and a lottery. The final financial breakthrough only came after the Zeppelin LZ4 crashed in 1908 at Echterdingen. The crash sparked public interest in the development of the airships. A subsequent collection campaign raised 6.5 million German marks and the money was used to create the 'Luftschiffbau-Zeppelin GmbH' and a Zeppelin foundation.[24]

The same year the military administration bought the LZ3 and put it to use as the renamed Z1. Starting in 1909, Zeppelins also were used in civilian aviation. Up until 1914 the German Aviation Association (*Deutsche Luftschiffahrtsgesellschaft* or DELAG) transported 37,250 people on over 1600 flights without an incident.[25] Within a few short years the zeppelin revolution began creating the age of air transportation.

Other aircraft

- 1899 unrealised plans for a paddlewheel aeroplane[19]
- 1912 financial support of Flugzeugbau Friedrichshafen which was to supply 850 aeroplanes 1917/1918;[19]
- 1914 commissions Claude Dornier to develop flying boats[19]
- 1914 founds Versuchsbau Gotha-Ost with Robert Bosch which built a number of Riesenflugzeug (giant aircraft) such as the Zeppelin-Staaken R.VI[19]

Legacy

Count Zeppelin died 1917, before the end of World War I. He therefore did not witness either the provisional shutdown of the Zeppelin project due to the Treaty of Versailles or the second resurgence of the zeppelins under his successor → Hugo Eckener. Unfinished WWII German aircraft carrier *Graf Zeppelin* and airships LZ 127 and LZ 130 *Graf Zeppelin* were named after him.

The British rock group Led Zeppelin's name derives from his airship as well. His granddaughter, Countess Eva Von Zeppelin, even once threatened to sue Led Zeppelin for illegal use of their family name while performing in Copenhagen.[26]

In the *Monty Python's Flying Circus* skit, "The Golden Age of Ballooning" (from episode 40), Count Zeppelin was featured. He became outraged at suggestions that his airship was just a balloon and that he was thinking of naming it after Bismarck. The offending parties (including von Bülow and Tirpitz) were hurled out of the zeppelin, crashing through the roof of a house.

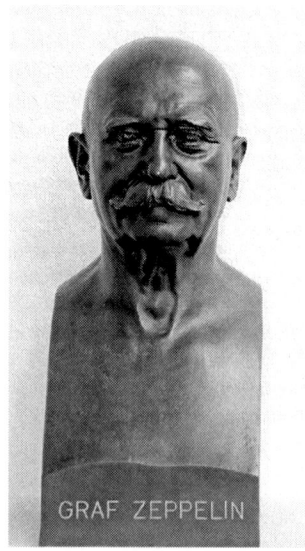

Bust of Zeppelin in AERONAUTICUM at Nordholz

See also

- → Airship
- Zeppelin
- Hindenburg disaster
- Timeline of hydrogen technologies

References

- Dooley, Sean C. 2004. The Development of Material-Adapted Structural Form [69] - Part II: Appendices [70]. THÈSE NO 2986 (2004), École Polytechnique Fédérale de Lausanne
- Eckener, Hugo. 1938. Count Zeppelin: The Man and His Work, translated by Leigh Fanell, London -- Massie Publishing Company, Ltd. -- (ASIN: B00085KPWK) (online extract pages 155-157, 210-211 [27])
- Lehmann, Ernst A.; Mingos, Howard. 1927. The Zeppelins. The Development of the Airship, with the Story of the Zepplins Air Raids in the World War. Chapter I GERMAN AIRSHIPS PREPARE FOR WAR [28]

Further reading

- Vömel, Alexander (1909-1933). *Graf Ferdinand von Zeppelin. Ein Mann der Tat.*

External links

- Ferdinand von Zeppelin [29] in the German National Library catalogue **(German)**
- "Biographie: Ferdinand Graf von Zeppelin, 1838-1917 [30]" (in German). Deutschen Historischen Museums. Retrieved 2009-09-12.
- Michael "Walter" Walz. "Stuttgart im Bild - Ferdinand Graf von Zeppelin [31]" (in German). Deutschen Historischen Museums. Retrieved 2009-09-12. (Gravestone in Stuttgart, biography and images)

References

[1] (in German) *Katalog der Deutschen Nationalbibliothek* (http://d-nb.info/gnd/118636545), , retrieved 2009-04-04
[2] (in German) *Stuttgart im Bild - Ferdinand Graf von Zeppelin* (http://www.stuttgart-im-bild.de/html/ferdinand_graf_von_zeppelin.html), , retrieved 2009-04-04
[3] Regarding personal names: *Graf* is a title, translated as *Count*, not a first or middle name. The female form is *Gräfin*. When "Graf" or its English translation "Count" is used, it is correct to omit the "von." Thus, "Ferdinand von Zeppelin", but "Graf Zeppelin" and "Count Zeppelin".
[4] *Zeppelin Biographie* (http://www.uni-konstanz.de/FuF/Philo/Geschichte/Zeppelin/english/bio.htm), , retrieved 2009-04-04
[5] Editors of German Wikipedia (http://de.wikipedia.org/w/index.php?title=Ferdinand_Graf_von_Zeppelin&oldid=47289919)
[6] *RootsWeb: GEN-DE-L Re: Zeppelin and Brandenstein family* (http://archiver.rootsweb.ancestry.com/th/read/GEN-DE/2002-05/1020898890), , retrieved 2009-04-04
[7] Lehmann
[8] (in German) *Lebenslauf von Graf Zeppelin* (http://www.hirschbergschule.de/ausfluege/ausflug7b/ausflug7bseite4.htm), , retrieved 2009-04-04
[9] *Zeppelin Biographie* (http://www.uni-konstanz.de/FuF/Philo/Geschichte/Zeppelin/english/lebensdaten.htm), , retrieved 2009-04-04
[10] Eckener 1938. pages 155-157
[11] Dooley A.176
[12] Dooley A.177
[13] Dooley A.178
[14] Dooley A.179
[15] Dooley A.181
[16] Dooley A.187
[17] Dooley A.188
[18] Dooley A.190
[19] Ernst-Heinrich Hirschel, Horst Prem, Gero Madelung (2004). *Aeronautical Research in Germany: From Lilienthal Until Today*. Springer. pp. 25-26. ISBN 354040645X. "ISBN 9783540406457"

[20] Dooley A.193-A.194
[21] Dooley A.183
[22] Eckener 1938. pages 210-211. "It is obvious at the first glance that the Zeppelin ship had nothing but its aluminium in common with the Schwarz machine, not to mention that Count Zeppelin had fixed the essential features long before Schwarz' ship appeared."
[23] Dooley A.191
[24] Dooley A.200
[25] Lehmann Chapter I "All told, 37,250 passengers had been carried, 1,600 flights made, 3,200 hours spent in the air and 90,000 miles flown without accident"
[26] Led Zeppelin - Official Website (http://ledzeppelin.com/show/february-28-1970) at ledzeppelin.com
[27] http://spot.colorado.edu/~dziadeck/airship/schwartz.htm
[28] http://www.hydrogencommerce.com/zepplins/zeppelin1.htm
[29] http://d-nb.info/gnd/118636545
[30] http://www.dhm.de/lemo/html/biografien/ZeppelinFerdinand/index.html
[31] http://www.stuttgart-im-bild.de/html/ferdinand_graf_von_zeppelin.html

Graf

Graf is a historical German noble title equal in rank to a **count** (derived from the Latin *Comes*, with a history of its own) or a British earl (an Anglo-Saxon title akin to the Viking title Jarl). A derivation ultimately from the Greek verb *graphein* 'to write' may be fanciful: Paul the Deacon wrote in Latin ca 790: "the count of the Bavarians that they call *gravio* who governed Bauzanum and other strongholds..." (*Historia gentis Langobardorum*, V.xxxvi); this may be read to make the term a Germanic one, but by then using Latin terms was quite common.

Since August 1919, in Germany, **Graf** and all other titles are considered as a part of the name.[1] The comital title **Graf** has of course also been used by German-speakers (as official or vernacular language), also in Austria and other Habsburg crown lands (mainly Slavic and Hungary), in Liechtenstein and much of Switzerland.

- A Graf (Count) ruled over a territory known as a *Grafschaft*, literally 'countship' (also rendered as 'county').
- The comital titles awarded in the Holy Roman Empire often related to the jurisdiction or domain of responsibility and represented special concessions of authority or rank. Only the more important titles remained in use until modern times. Many Counts were titled *Graf* without any additional qualification.
- For a list of the titles of the rank of Count etymologically related to Graf (and for other equivalents) see article Count.

List of nobiliary titles containing the term *graf*

Some are approximately of comital rank, some higher, some lower. The more important ones are treated in separate articles (follow the links); a few minor, rarer ones only in sections below.

German	English	Comment/ etymology
Markgraf	*Margrave* (only continental) and (younger) *Marquess* or *Marquis*	Mark: march (border province) + Graf
Landgraf	*Landgrave*	*Land* (country) + Graf
Reichsgraf	*Count of the Empire*	Reich i.e., (the Holy Roman) Empire + Graf
Gefürsteter Graf	*Princely Count*	German verb for "to make into a Reichsfürst" + Graf
Pfalzgraf	*Count Palatine* or *Palsgrave* (the latter is archaic in English)	*Pfalz* (palatial estate, Palatinate) + Graf
Rheingraf	*Rhinegrave*	Rhein (river Rhine) + Graf
Burggraf	*Burgrave*	*Burg* (castle, burgh) + Graf

Altgraf	Altgrave	*Alt* (old) + Graf (very rare)
Freigraf	*Free Count*	*Frei* = free (allodial?) + Graf; both a feudal title of comital rank *and* a more technical office
Wildgraf	*Wildgrave*	*Wild* (game or wilderness) + Graf
Raugraf	*Raugrave*	*Rau* (raw, uninhabited, wilderness) + Graf
Vizegraf	*Viscount*	*Vize* = vice- (substitute) + Graf

Reichsgraf, Gefürsteter Graf

A *Reichsgraf* was a nobleman whose title of *count* was conferred or confirmed by the Holy Roman Emperor, and literally meant "count of the (Holy Roman) Empire". Since the feudal era any count whose territory lay within the Empire, was under the immediate jurisdiction of the Emperor, and exercised a shared vote in the Reichstag came to be considered a member of the "upper nobility" (*Hochadel*) in Germany, along with princes (*Fursten*), dukes (*Herzogen*), electors, and the emperor himself. [2] A count who was not a *Reichsgraf* was apt to possess only a "mediate" fief (*Afterlehen*) — he was subject to an immediate prince of the empire, such as a duke or elector.

However, the Holy Roman Emperors also occasionally granted the title of *Reichsgraf* to subjects and foreigners who did not possess and were not granted immediate territories -- or, sometimes, any territory at all.[3] Such titles were purely honorific. In English, *Reichsgraf* is usually translated simply as *count* and is combined with a territorial suffix (e.g. Count of Holland, Count Reuss, or a surname Count Fugger, Count von Browne. But even after the abolition of the Holy Roman Empire in 1806, the *Reichsgrafen* retained precedence above other counts in Germany. Those who had been quasi-sovereign until German mediatisation retained, until 1918, status and privileges pertaining to members of reigning dynasties.

A *gefürsteter Graf* (in English, *princely count*) is a *Reichsgraf* who has been made *Reichsgraf* by an act of the king, as opposed to one whose ancestors have held this privilege since the High Middle Ages.

Notable *Reichsgrafen* included:

- Castell
- Fugger
- Henneberg, a title merged into the imperial dignity
- Leiningen
- Nassau-Weilburg since 26 September 1366 (previously, simply *Graf*)
- Pappenheim
- Tyrol as a dominion of the Austrian crown
- Stolberg

A complete list of *Reichsgrafen* as of 1792 can be found in the List of Reichstag participants (1792).

Landgrave

A *Landgraf* or *Landgrave* was a nobleman of comital rank in feudal Germany whose jurisdiction stretched over a sometimes quite considerable territory. The title survived from the times of the Holy Roman Empire. The status of a landgrave was often associated with sovereign rights and decision-making greater than those of a simple Graf (Count), but carried no legal prerogatives.

Landgraf occasionally continued in use as the subsidiary title of such nobility as the Grand Duke of Saxe-Weimar, who functioned as the *Landgrave* of Thuringia in the first decade of the 20th century; but the title fell into disuse after World War I. The jurisdiction of a landgrave was a *Landgrafschaft* landgraviate and the wife of a landgrave was a *Landgräfin* or landgravine.

Examples: Landgrave of Thuringia, Landgrave of Hesse (later split in Hesse-Kassel and Hesse-Darmstadt), Landgrave of Leuchtenberg.

Gefürsteter Landgraf

A combination of Landgraf and Gefürsteter Graf (both above). Example: Leuchtenberg, later a duchy.

Burgrave / Viscount

A *Burggraf*, or *Burgrave*, was a 12th and 13th century military and civil judicial governor of a castle (compare Castellan, *Custos*, Keeper) of the town it dominated and of its immediate surrounding countryside. His jurisdiction was a *Burggrafschaft*, burgraviate.

Later the title became ennobled and hereditary with its own domain.

Example: Burgrave of Nuremberg.

It occupies the same relative rank as titles rendered in purist German by *Vizegraf*, in Dutch as *Burggraaf* or in English as *Viscount* (Latin: *Vicecomes*), in origin also a deputy of a Count, as the burgrave dwelt usually in a castle or fortified town. Soon many became hereditary and *almost-a-Count*, ranking just below the 'full' Counts, but above a *Freiherr* (Baron).

It was also often used as a courtesy title by the heir to a *Graf*.

Rhinegrave, Wildgrave, Raugrave, Altgrave

Unlike the other comital titles, the titles of Rhinegrave, Wildgrave (Waldgrave), Raugrave, and Altgrave are not generic titles. Instead, each is linked to one specific countship. By rank, these unusually named counts are equivalent to other counts.

- "Rhinegrave" (German *Rheingraf*) was the title of the count of the Rheingau, a county located between Wiesbaden and Lorch on the right bank of the Rhine. Their castle was known as the Rheingrafenstein. After the Rhinegraves inherited the Wildgraviate (see below) and parts of the Countship of Salm, they called themselves Wild- and Rhinegraves of Salm. [4]
- When the Nahegau (a countship named after the river Nahe) split into two parts in 1113, the counts of the two parts called themselves Wildgraves and Raugraves, respectively. They were named after the geographic properties of their territories: Wildgrave (*Wildgraf*), in Latin *comes sylvanus*, after *Wald* ("forest"), Raugrave (*Raugraf*), in Latin *comes hirsutus*, after the rough (i.e., mountainous) terrain. [5]
- The first Raugrave was Count Emich I (died 1172). The dynasty died out in the 18th century. The title was taken over after Elector Palatine Karl Ludwig I purchased the estates, and after 1667 was owned by the children from the Elector's bigamous (morganatic) second marriage to Karl's wife, Marie Louise von Degenfeld. [6]
- Altgrave (German *Altgraf*, "old count") was a title used by the counts of Lower Salm to distinguish themselves from the Wild- and Rhinegraves of Upper Salm, since Lower Salm was the senior branch of the family.

Other uses

Furthermore, the term -graf occurs in various office titles which did not attain nobiliary status, but were either held as a sinecure by nobleman or courtiers, or by those who remained functional officials, such as the Deichgraf (in a polder management organism).

See also

- German nobility
- History of Germany
- Holy Roman Emperor
- Reichstag (institution)
- List of German monarchs
- List of states in the Holy Roman Empire
- Nobility
- Sendgraf
- List of rulers of Austria

Sources and references

(incomplete)

- WorldStatesmen: see every modern state; here Germany/Holy Roman Empire [7]

[1] Weimar Constitution Article 109, sentence 2
[2] Velde, François (2008-02-13). " Heraldica.org (http://www.heraldica.org/topics/national/hre.htm#Evolution)". *The Holy Roman Empire*. . Retrieved 2008-03-04.
[3] Velde, François (2008-02-13). " Heraldica.org (http://www.heraldica.org/topics/national/hre.htm#Evolution)". *The Holy Roman Empire*. . Retrieved 2008-03-04.
[4] Rheingraf at Meyers Konversationslexikon, 1888 (http://susi.e-technik.uni-ulm.de:8080/Meyers2/seite/werk/meyers/band/13/seite/0780/meyers_b13_s0780.html)
[5] Raugraf at Meyers Konversationslexikon, 1888 (http://susi.e-technik.uni-ulm.de:8080/Meyers2/seite/werk/meyers/band/13/seite/0605/meyers_b13_s0605.html#Raugraf)
[6] Raugraf at wissen.de (http://www.wissen.de/wde/generator/wissen/ressorts/geschichte/index,page=1221956.html)
[7] http://www.worldstatesmen.org/Germany.html#Holy%20Roman%20Empire

External links

- Lexikon article "Raugraf" (http://www.wissen.de/wde/generator/wissen/ressorts/geschichte/index,page=1221956.html)

Hugo Eckener

Dr. Hugo Eckener (10 August 1868–14 August 1954)[1] [2] [3] was the manager of the Luftschiffbau Zeppelin during the inter-war years, and was commander of the famous → *Graf Zeppelin* for most of its record-setting flights, including the first airship flight around the world, making him the most successful airship commander in history. He was also responsible for the construction of the most successful type of airships of all time. An anti-Nazi who was invited to campaign as a moderate in the German presidential elections,[1] [4] [5] he was blacklisted by that regime and eventually sidelined.

Background

Eckener was born in Flensburg as the first child of Johann Christoph Eckener from Bremen and Anna Lange, daughter of a shoemaker.[1] As a youth he was judged an "indifferent student",[1] [2] and he spent summers sailing and winters ice skating.[1]

Hugo Eckener in 1924

Nevertheless, by 1892 under Professor Wilhelm Wundt Eckner had earned a doctorate "magna cum laude"[1] in what today might be deemed experimental psychology.[2] at the University of Leipzig.

Eckener then began his military service in the Infantry Regiment 86 in Flensburg.[1]

Eckener's early career was as a journalist and editor; by August 1893 he was working for the *Flensburger Nachrichten*[1] ; in October 1897 he married Johanna, daughter of the publisher-family Maaß;[1] later he became a correspondent for the Frankfurter Zeitung[2] in 1905 and 1906, whilst writing a book on the social effects of capitalism.

Pre-war airship activities

Asked to cover the first flights of the LZ1 and LZ2, Eckener was critical of both airships' marginal performances, but praised Count → Ferdinand von Zeppelin's dedication to his cause. Because several scientists and engineers had criticized his airship plans, the Count sought to speak to his critic and Eckener was so impressed by him that during October 1908 he agreed to be a part-time publicist for the Zeppelin Company.[1] He became extremely interested in airships, and joined the company on a full-time basis.

His aptitude at flying was noticed early on in his career, and he became an airship captain, obtaining his airship license in 1911.[3] [5] However, when Eckener attempted his first flight on 16 May 1911 in the LZ 8, christened *Deutschland II*, he decided to launch in a strong wind which pushed the craft into the hangar wall, damaging it seriously.[6] Nonetheless, he became a very successful airshipman.

World War I

Eckener was responsible for training most of Germany's airship pilots both during[6] and after World War I. Despite his protestations, he was not allowed on operational missions due to his important value as an instructor.

Head of the Zeppelin Company

After the War, Eckener succeeded Count → Ferdinand von Zeppelin, who had died on 8 March 1917. After considerable conflict with Zeppelin's business manager, Alfred Colesman, who wanted to replace the production of airships with production of other (and likely more profitable) products, Eckener was able to keep the Zeppelin factory at Friedrichshafen on Bodensee (Lake Constance) in Wurttemberg, southern Germany, from being retooled. Colesman left the company soon afterwards.

Eckener (marked with an x) test flying the LZ 126 in August before delivery to the United States in October 1924

The Treaty of Versailles had forbidden Germans to construct airships of the size needed[5] to operate the profitable trans-Atlantic service that was Eckener's goal. However, after much skilful lobbying, he persuaded the US and German governments to allow the company to build LZ 126, later rechristened the *USS Los Angeles (ZR-3)*, for the US Navy as part of Germany's war reparations. Eckener himself captained the airship on its delivery flight to Lakehurst, New Jersey.[1] [5] The *Los Angeles* became the longest-serving rigid airship ever operated by the US Navy.

The golden age of the rigid airship

Refused funds by the impecunious Weimar government, Eckener and his colleagues began a nationwide fund-raising lecture tour in order to commence construction of → *Graf Zeppelin*, which became the most successful rigid airship ever built.

The first flight to America was fraught with drama; on the outbound flight the airship was nearly lost after becoming caught in a severe storm. Fabric was ripped off the left fin. The ship was saved only by Eckener's skilled piloting and the courage of his son, Knut Eckener, and other crew members who climbed out onto the fin to repair the damage.[7] Upon arrival in America, a country which Eckener grew to love, he and the crew were subject to the first of two New York ticker tape parades.

Eckener captained *Graf Zeppelin* during most of its record-setting flights, including a flight to the Arctic and a flight around the world - the only such flight by an airship, and the second by an aircraft of any type.

Russian polar researcher Rudol'f Lazarevic Samojlovic (left) prior to leading the → Graf Zeppelin's scientific polar flight, with Eckener in Friedrichshafen, July 1931

A master of publicity as well as a master airship captain, Eckener used the *Graf Zeppelin* to establish the Zeppelin as a symbol of German pride and engineering.

After the Zeppelin flights (1928 America, 1929 round the world and 1931 Arctic) the public treated Eckener as a national hero.[5] During the early 1930s, Eckener was one of the most well-known and respected figures in Weimar

Republic Germany.

In 1932 Eckener had intended to run against Hitler[4] for president,[1] [5] and this angered the Nazi party.[8] In supposed anger and fear of Eckener, Hitler's defacto deputy, Hermann Esser, once called him the "director of the flying white sausage".[4] He was encouraged to campaign for the presidency to oppose the National Socialist German Workers Party.[6] Contrary to popular belief, Eckener accepted to campaign for president, but stopped when Paul Von Hindenburg campaigned for President again.

Sidelined

The National Socialists came to power in January 1933. An arrest of Eckener in 1933 was intended but blocked by Hindenberg. Hitler met Eckener only one time, in July 1933, but the two barely spoke.[1]

Eckener did not make any secret of his dislike of the Nazis[8] and the disastrous events he foresaw. He criticised the regime frequently, and refused to allow the Nazis to use the large hangars at Frankfurt for a rally. Eventually the Nazis declared Eckener to be *persona non grata* and his name was no longer allowed to appear in print.

During his many years as manager of airship operations, Eckener always made safety his absolute priority. With Eckener's management, the Zeppelin company had a perfect safety record with no passenger ever sustaining a serious injury on any of the more than 1 million air miles that the rigid airships flew, until the Hindenburg disaster of 1937.

During the 1930s the Nazi government nationalized the Zeppelin operation. The Nazis sidelined Eckener in favour of men who were somewhat more compliant with their wishes. In their haste to please the Nazi regime, these newly promoted airshipmen did not always obey Eckener's well-proven safety procedures. For example, the maiden voyage of the Hindenburg nearly resulted in disaster when Captain Ernst Lehmann brought the ship out in strong winds in order to undertake a Nazi propaganda flight. The ship was damaged severely, and there was an argument between Eckener and Lehman.

Hugo Eckener was in Graz, Austria when he heard news of the Hindenburg disaster of 6 May 1937. In the official inquiry he concluded that a static spark ignited leaking hydrogen in the aft section of the ship. The leak would have been caused by a sharp turn, which he believed caused a wire to break and rip a gas cell.

After the destruction of the *Hindenburg*, the nearly-completed → LZ-130 *Graf Zeppelin* was redesigned as a helium-filled ship, although, owing to geo-political considerations, the American helium was not available. Thus the ship never began commercial service. However, with the command of Captain Albert Sammt, the ship performed a number of controversial espionage flights over Great Britain.[9]

Eckener, however, had by this time little influence on the Zeppelin Company. He survived World War II despite his disagreements with the Nazis. Post war, he was involved with a plan by the Goodyear Zeppelin Corporation to build large rigid airships. However this did not happen.

In 1945 Johannes Weyl and Eckener co-found the *Südkurier* regional newspaper and Eckener started writing for German-French co-operation.[1] [3]

In November 1945 Eckener was confronted with the charge of collaboration with Nazi Germany. In 1947 the French occupying powers fined him 100,000 German Reichsmarks. Many personalities lobbied for Eckener's rehabilitation.[10] The judgement was rejected in July 1948 and Eckener was rehabilitated.[1]

Eckener's home town of Flensburg had a Danish-oriented majority in its council since 1945, with a goal of Danish unification. Eckener remained active in local politics campaigning for a German majority in Flensburg, while at the same time, during a "thundering" one hour speech in 1951, warning against small-mindedness in border concerns.[1]

Eckener died in Friedrichshafen on 14 August 1954 just after his 86th birthday.[1]

Legacy

Eckener was responsible for many innovative aviation developments, notably the trans-Atlantic passenger services offered by the airships *Graf Zeppelin* and *Hindenburg*. Together with his chief designer, Dr. Ludwig Dürr, he was responsible for developing the rigid airship to near-perfection for the time.

Since his death his achievements have been remembered by airship enthusiasts and historians. However, the town of Friedrichshafen, scene of his many triumphant homecomings in *Graf Zeppelin*, has recognised his memory by naming a large new conference centre after him.

Das Haus des Glockenspiels in Bremen's Böttcherstraße displays this panel as part of 10 from Bernhard Hoetger's 1934 "ocean-crossing" set

Bibliography

Eckener wrote or contributed to 24 publications,[11] including two books in English:[12]

> Eckener, Hugo: Count Zeppelin. The Man and his Work. London: Massie Publishing Company, Ltd. 1938.
>
> Eckener, Hugo: My Zeppelins. London: Putnam 1958.

See also

- Graf Zeppelin
- Hindenburg
- Zeppelin
- → List of Zeppelins
- → Ferdinand von Zeppelin

References

- Hugo Eckener [13] in the German National Library catalogue (**German**)
- Schwensen, Broder (August 1996). "Hugo Eckener Leben und Tat des Flensburger Luftschiffers 1868 - 1954 [14]" (in German). "zusammengestellt und kommentiert vom Städtischen Archivdirektor Dr. Broder Schwensen, Flensburg August 1996"
- de Syon, Guillaume (2002). *Zeppelin!: Germany and the Airship, 1900–1939*. Johns Hopkins University Press. ISBN 9780801867347. ISBN 0801867347.
- Nustede, Nina. "Englische Auswahlbibliographie zu Zeppelin [15]" (in English) (PDF). Retrieved 2009-10-04. - select English-language bibliographic list on the Zeppelin
- "ostsee.de Infocenter - Hugo Eckener [16]" (in German). ostsee.de. Retrieved 2009-10-04. - short biography
- Adam, Thomas; David Murphy (2005). *Germany and the Americas: culture, politics, and history; Germany and the Americas: culture, politics, and history; Transatlantic relations series; Volume 1 of Germany and the Americas: Culture, Politics, and History : a Multidisciplinary Encyclopedia*. ABC-CLIO. pp. 289-290. ISBN 9781851096282. ISBN 1851096280.
- "Glossen; Erscheint Nach Bedarf [17]" (in German). *Sozialdemokratischer Pressedienst*. Social Democratic Party of Germany. 1932-02-18. pp. 11-12. Retrieved 2009-10-04. "Esser sorgt vor. Der Nazimann Esser hat einer Zorn auf Dr. Eckener gefasst, weil er für Hindenburg eingetreten ist. Esser fürchtet Eckener auch noch, weil er einmal als Kandidat gegen Hitler gennant wurde. Kan man wissen, was kommt noch? Also gedachte Esser, Herrn

Eckener vorsorglich durch einen fürchterlichen Schlag zu erledigen. Da nannte er ihn in einer Münchener Versammlung den "Direktor der fliegenden Weisswurst"." - scans of original Social Democratic Party of Germany press publication, rough translation: Esser worries. The Nazi Esser fixed his anger against Eckener because he has stood for Hindenburg. Esser still fears Eckener because he was once named as a candidate against Hitler. Who knows what will come? Therefore Esser intended that Eckener should be "finished" (stopped? killed?) by a frightful stroke/strike. In a Munich meeting he called him "the director of the flying white sausage".

- Brandes, Markus. "Ada English - Autographs of Count Zeppelin and Hugo Eckener [18]". Archived from the original [19] on 2007-11-28.
- Sammt, Albert. 1988. *Mein Leben für den Zeppelin*, Verlag Pestalozzi Kinderdorf Wahlwies 1988, ISBN 3-921583-02-0 - pages 167-168 [20] extract covering LZ 130's spying trip from 2 to 4 August 1939, (German) (pdf)

Further reading

Books

- Botting, Douglas. *Dr. Eckener's Dream Machine* (2001) Harper Collins ISBN 0-00-257191-9
- Dick, Harold G. / Robinson, Douglas H.: The Golden Age of the Great Passenger Airships. Graf Zeppelin & Hindenburg. Washington D.C./London 2nd edition 1987.
- Meyer, Henry Cord: Airshipmen, Businessmen and Politics 1890 – 1940. Washington/London: Smithsonian Institution Press/Airlife Publishing Ltd. 1991. with chapters: Eckener's Struggle to Save the Airship for Germany, 1919-1929; Politics, Personality, and Technology: Airships in the Manipulations of Dr. Hugo Eckener and Lord Thomson, 1919-1930.
- Payne, Lee: Lighter than Air. An Illustrated History of the Airship. London: Thomas Yoseloff Ltd 1977. with chapter: Hugo Eckener and the Graf Zeppelin.
- Robinson, Douglas H. *Giants in the Sky: A History of the Rigid Airship* (1973) University of Washington Press ISBN 0854291458
- Vaeth, J. Gordon. *Graf Zeppelin - The Adventures of an Aerial Globetrotter* (1959) Muller, London
- Whitehouse, Arthur George Joseph. *The Zeppelin Fighters* (1966) Robert Hale Limited ISBN 0-7091-0544-4

Online

- Media related to Hugo Eckener at Wikimedia Commons
- Grossman, Daniel. "Airships: A Hindenburg and Zeppelin History Site / Hugo Eckener [21]". Airships.net. Retrieved 2009-10-06. illustrated brief biography
- "Airship - Knut Eckener [22]". summitmemory.org. Retrieved 2009-10-06. "Knut Eckener and the zeppelin mascot, "Vee-Dol" a chow puppy who was carried on the German zeppelins to ward off bad luck." - photograph
- "Airship - Knut Eckener [23]". summitmemory.org. Retrieved 2009-10-06. "A portrait of Knut Eckener." - photograph

References

[1] Schwensen
[2] Thomas Adam. p. 289
[3] ostsee.de
[4] Social Democratic Party of Germany 18 February 1932 p. 12
[5] Thomas Adam. p. 290
[6] Brandes 2004
[7] Channel 4 History. The Airships (http://www.channel4.com/history/microsites/H/history/a-b/airships2.html)
[8] de Syon, p.176 "opponent of the economic policy of autarky and of the regime's Jewish policies" ... "incensed by the new flag order"
[9] Sammt 1988
[10] de Syon, p.207 "convicted of helping the war effort ... lost civil privileges in 1948 for five years ... 100,000-mark fine"
[11] German National Library
[12] Nina Nustede
[13] http://d-nb.info/gnd/118528750
[14] http://www.flensburg-online.de/geschich/eckener1.html
[15] http://www.zeppelin-museum.de/uploads/media/Zeppelin_Englisch.pdf
[16] http://www.ostsee.de/flensburg/hugo-eckener.html
[17] http://library.fes.de/spdpdalt/19320218.pdf
[18] http://web.archive.org/web/20071128160400/http://www.autogramme.ch/html/joomla/index.php?option=com_content&task=view&id=2&Itemid=29
[19] http://www.autogramme.ch/html/joomla/index.php?option=com_content&task=view&id=2&Itemid=29
[20] http://www.luftschiffharry.de/doku/LZ_130_Spionagefahrt.pdf
[21] http://www.airships.net/hugo-eckener
[22] http://www.summitmemory.org/cdm4/item_viewer.php?CISOROOT=/fulton&CISOPTR=175&CISOBOX=1&REC=16
[23] http://www.summitmemory.org/cdm4/item_viewer.php?CISOROOT=/fulton&CISOPTR=152&CISOBOX=1&REC=17

Maybach

MAYBACH	
Type	division of Daimler AG
Founded	1909
Founder(s)	Wilhelm Maybach
Headquarters	Stuttgart, Germany
Industry	Automotive
Products	Luxury vehicles
Parent	Daimler AG
Website	Maybach [1]

Maybach-Motorenbau GmbH (German pronunciation: [ˈmaɪbax]) (founded 1909) is a German luxury car manufacturer. It was founded in 1909 by Wilhelm Maybach with his son Karl Maybach as director. The company was originally a subsidiary of Luftschiffbau Zeppelin GmbH and was itself known as "Luftfahrzeug-Motoreinbau GmbH" (literally "Aircraft Engine Installation Company") until 1918. Today, the brand is owned by Daimler AG and based in Stuttgart.

Maybach SW 42, 1939

1909–1940: Early history

Maybach has historic roots through the involvement of Wilhelm Maybach, who was the technical director of the Daimler-Motoren-Gesellschaft. The company originally developed and manufactured diesel and gas engines for Zeppelins, and then rail cars. The Maybach Mb.IVa was used in aircraft and airships of World War I.

Captured Maybach T3 Assault Gun (Sturmgeschütz III), made on the basis of medium tank Maybach T3 (Panzer III). National Museum of Military History (Bulgaria)

Early poster with double M logo

The company first built an experimental car in 1919, with the first production model introduced two years later at the Berlin Motor Show. Between 1921 and 1940, the company produced various classic opulent vehicles. The company also continued to build heavy duty diesel engines for marine and rail purposes.

Maybach contributed to the German fascist war effort in World War II by producing the engines for many mobile artilleries and tanks such as Jagdpanther, Panther and Tiger tanks with the Maybach HL230. After the war the factory performed some repair work, but automotive production was never restarted, and some 20 years later, the company was renamed into MTU Friedrichshafen.

1997–present: revival

In 1997, Mercedes-Benz presented at the Tokyo Motorshow a luxury concept car under the name **Mercedes-Benz Maybach** (V12, 5987 cc, 550 hp). Mercedes-Benz decided to develop it; however, Mercedes made the decision to market the car under the sole brand name of Maybach.

Maybach was therefore revived as a brand in the early 2000s, with the production of the new model in two sizes — the Maybach 57 and the Maybach 62. The numbers are equal to the lengths of the automobiles in decimetres. In 2005, the new 57S was added, sporting a 6.0L V12 bi-turbo engine, producing 604 bhp (450 kW) and 737 lb·ft (999 N·m) of torque, and featuring various cosmetic touches.

The company offers various options for customers to personalise their vehicles, and provides various equipment combinations.

Maybach 62

To promote the new Maybach line, Mercedes-Benz has tapped public figures to act as brand ambassadors, including Maybach heir Ulrich Schmid-Maybach and golfer Nick Faldo.[2] [3]

Models

Pre-war

- 1919 Maybach W1: Test car based on a Mercedes chassis
- 1921 Maybach W3: First Maybach, shown at Berlin Motor Show. Featured a 70 hp (52 kW) 5.7L inline six.
- 1926 Maybach W5: 7L inline six, 120 hp (89 kW)
- 1929 Maybach 12: V12 precursor to DS7/8
- 1930 Maybach DSH: Doppel-Sechs-Halbe ("half a twelve cylinder") 1930-37
- 1930 Maybach DS7 Zeppelin: 7L V12, 150 hp (112 kW)
- 1931 Maybach W6: Same engine as W5, longer wheelbase. 1931-33
- 1931 Maybach DS8 Zeppelin: 8L V12, 200 hp (150 kW)
- 1934 Maybach W6 DSG: Featuring a twin overdrive transmission system.
- 1935 Maybach SW35: 3.5L 140 hp (104 kW) I6

Several Maybach 57 and 62 models at the 2005 Concours d'Elegance in Pebble Beach, CA.

- 1936 Maybach SW38: 3.8L 140 hp (104 kW) I6
- 1939 Maybach SW42: 4.2L 140 hp (104 kW) I6
- 1945 Maybach JW61: 3.8L 145 hp (108 kW) I6

W2 were the 5.7L inline six engines built for and ordered by Spyker. Not all were purchased, and Karl had to build cars featuring the engines to offset costs.

Around 1800 Maybachs were built before WW2.

Post-revival

- 2002 Maybach 57 and 62
- 2005 Maybach Exelero (prototype shown at the IAA in Frankfurt)
- 2005 Maybach 57S (the S standing for Special rather than Sport)
- 2006 Maybach 62S
- 2007 Maybach 62 Landaulet
- 2009 Maybach 57 Zeppelin and Maybach 62 Zeppelin

Performance

Maybach Exelero at the Concours d'Elegance

The Maybach 57 accelerates from 0 to 60 mph (0 to 97 km/h) in about 5.1 seconds; the Maybach 62 and 57 S, about 4.8 seconds; the Maybach 62 S, 4.5 seconds, and the Landaulet, 4.5 seconds. Though not extraordinary by today's sports-car standards, such acceleration is impressive for cars weighing well over 6,000 pounds. Maybachs in general are extremely powerful: the 57 has 518 bhp (386 kW; 525 PS); the 57 S, 559 bhp (417 kW; 567 PS); the 62, 570 bhp (425 kW; 578 PS); the 62 S, 612 bhp (456 kW; 620 PS), and the Landaulet, 633 bhp (472 kW; 642 PS).

Amenities

Standard features of all Maybach models include, but are not limited to, a navigation system w/voice recognition, air conditioning w/4-zone climate controls, power rear sunshade, rear-seat DVD entertainment system, interior air filter, front and rear seat massage, 24-speaker premium sound system, power tilt/telescopic heated wood/leather-wrapped steering wheel w/radio and climate controls, power trunk open/close, voice-activated AM/FM radio w/10-disc CD changer, keyless start, heated front and rear seats, cooled front seats, power panoramic sunroof, adaptive cruise control, premium leather upholstery, 18-way power front seats, 14-way power rear seats, heated cupholders, rearview camera, iPod adapter, wireless cell phone link, outside-temperature indicator, universal garage door opener, and night vision. Options for the Maybach 57 and 57S and standard for the Maybach 62, 62S, and Landaulet include 18-way power rear seats (replacing 14-way), 5-zone climate controls (replacing 4-zone), power side sunshades, cooled rear seats, wireless headphones, voice-activated power panoramic sunroof (replacing power panoramic sunroof), steering wheel mounted navigation controls, heated glass windows, and 30-speaker premium sound system (replacing 24-speaker).

Price

The base price of a 2009 Maybach 57 is $344,000; the Maybach 57 S, $381,000; the Maybach 62, $394,000; the Maybach 62 S, $430,000, and the Maybach Landaulet semi convertible, just under $470,000. The Maybach 57 Zeppelin is priced at Euro 406,000 ($580,000) and the 62 Zeppelin at Euro 473,200 ($677,000)[4]. The price of used vehicles varies based on mileage, condition, and other factors.

Future models

Three new models are expected, a 4-seat sedan derived from the Mercedes-Benz CLS-Class, a full-size luxury SUV derived from the GL-Class, and a smaller sedan, which would be sold for $250,000. Recently, they launched a Landaulet convertible like the Maybachs of old and this was first shown in Dubai[5]

With less than stellar sales expectations and heavy impact of 2008 financial crises, Daimler AG is considering cancelling the whole Maybach division. However, Daimler AG has been in talks with Aston-Martin to engineer and style the next generation of Maybach models along with the next generation of Lagonda models. Both are to be based on new Maybach chassis. No release date is given.

US Sales

US Calendar Year	Sales
2003[6]	166
2004	244
2005[7]	152
2006	146
2007[8]	156
2008	119

Initially, Daimler-Chrysler predicted annual sales of 2,000 global units with 50% coming from the United States. However such lofty sales expectations never materialized.[9] [10] In 2007 Mercedes bought back 29 US dealers, reducing the total from 71 to 42.[11]

See also

- List of German cars
- Wilhelm Maybach
- Maybach Foundation

External links

- Maybach Manufaktur [1]
- The Maybach Museum (in German) [12]
- A biography of Wilhelm Maybach (in German) [13]
- Technical information about Maybach engines in the *Tiger I* tank [14]
- Maybach Foundation [15]

References

[1] http://www.maybach-manufaktur.com/
[2] Ryono, Debra. The Maybach Hybrid. worth.com. 2009-01-04. URL:http://www.worth.com/Editorial/Thought-Leaders/Profiles/Profile-Maybach-April-May08.asp.Accessed: 2009-01-04. (Archived by WebCite at http://www.webcitation.org/5dakIZV1p)
[3] Hodzic, Muamer. Nick Faldo is the new Maybach brand ambassador. Benzinsider.com. 2009-03-08. URL:http://www.benzinsider.com/2007/03/nick-faldo-is-the-new-maybach-brand-ambassador/.Accessed: 2009-03-08. (Archived by WebCite at http://www.webcitation.org/5f8C5a1sA)
[4] Maybach Zeppelin: resurrection of the dead (http://autoreview.belproject.com/item/902)
[5] http://www.emercedesbenz.com/Apr07/26_A_Look_Ahead_Maybach_Discusses_Future_Plans_With_Automobile_Magazine.html
[6] 2004 Highest Year on Record for Mercedes-Benz USA (http://www.theautochannel.com/news/2005/01/04/313903.html)
[7] Mercedes-Benz Rings in the New Year with Record 2006 Sales (http://www.theautochannel.com/news/2007/01/03/032870.html)
[8] Mercedes-Benz USA's Sales Drop 32.1 Percent In December 2008 (http://www.emercedesbenz.com/Jan09/05_001548_Mercedes_Benz_USA_Sales_Drop_32_Percent_In_December_2008.html)
[9] DaimlerChrysler Turns Profit on $300,000 Maybach (http://www.edmunds.com/insideline/do/News/articleId=105149?mktcat=enabler&AID=10364102&PID=3179980&kw=N&synpartner=edmunds&mktid=cj260223)
[10] Can Maybach Be Mended? (http://automobile.automotive.com/5038/0705-maybach-future-plan/index.html)
[11] Mercedes-Benz buys back and closes 29 Maybach dealers (http://www.autoblog.com/2007/10/01/mercedes-benz-buys-back-and-closes-29-maybach-dealers/)
[12] http://www.automuseum-maybach.de/
[13] http://www.dhm.de/lemo/html/biografien/MaybachWilhelm/
[14] http://www.alanhamby.com/maybach.shtml
[15] http://www.maybach.org/

Buoyancy compensator (aviation)

The static buoyancy of → airships during a trip is not constant. It is therefore necessary to take measures to control the buoyancy and thus the altitude, the so-called **buoyancy compensation**.

Changes which have an effect on buoyancy

- Changes in air temperature (and thus the density of air)
- Changes in the lifting gas temperature (for example by heating of the hull by the sun).
- Accumulation of additional ballast (for example, precipitation or icing on the envelope)
- Changes in ballast (for example, during a flight maneuver or the dropping of ballast)
- Changes by consumption of fuel, especially in the large historic airships like the Zeppelins the problem of change in the buoyancy balance by consumption of fuel needed attention.

For example, the LZ 126 spent on the flight from Friedrichshafen to Lakehurst 23,000 kg gasoline and 1300 kg of oil (an average consumption of 290 kg/100 km). During the landing the airship had to release approximately 24,000 cubic meters of hydrogen to balance the ship to land it. An airship with the size of the LZ 129 Hindenburg spent on a flight from Frankfurt am Main to Lakehurst approximately 54 tonnes of diesel with a buoyancy equivalent of 48,000 cubic metres hydrogen which amounted for about a quarter of the used lifting gas at the start of the flight (200,000 cubic metres). After landing the jettisonised hydrogen was replaced with new hydrogen.

Compensation measures

- Particular use of the dynamic buoyancy, see lift and drag.
- Increasing buoyancy by dropping ballast. This is done mostly by the jettisoning of ballast water similar to the dropping of sandbags in ballooning.
- The reduction of buoyancy by jettisoning liftgas or adding ballast.
- Changing the density of the lifting gas by heating (more buoyancy) or cooling (less buoyancy).
- The use of vacuum/air buoyancy compensator tanks[1]
- The use of thrust vectoring using ducted fans or propellers.

The Zeppelin NT has no special facilities to offset the extra buoyancy by fuel consumption. Compensation takes place by using a start-weight that is higher than the buoyancy lifting level at the start and during the flight, the extra dynamic buoyancy needed for lift-off and flight is produced with engines. If during the trip the ship gets lighter than air caused by fuel consumption, the swivel engines are used for down pressure and landing. The relatively small size of the Zeppelin NT and a range of "only" 900 kilometers compared to the historical zeppelins allowed the waiver of a ballast extraction device.

Buoyancy compensation

With a Zeppelin two main strategies are pursued to avoid the jettisoning of lifting gas:

- 1. The use of a fuel with the same density as air and therefore no increase in buoyancy caused by consumption.
- 2. Adding water as ballast by extraction during the trip.

Fuel with a density close to air

Only gasses have a density similar or equal to the air.

Hydrogen

Different attempts were made on hydrogen airships, like the → LZ 127 and LZ 129 to use part of the lifting gas as a propellant without much success, later ships filled with helium lacked the option.

Blaugas

Around 1905 Blau gas was a common propellant for airships, it is named after its inventor the Augsburger chemist Hermann Blau who produced it in the Augsburger Blau gas plant. Various sources mention a mixture of liquefied propane and butane. In density it was 9% heavier than air. The Zeppelins used a different gas mixture of propylene, methane, butane, acetylene (ethine), butylene and hydrogen.

The → LZ 127 Graf Zeppelin had bi-fuel engines and could use gasoline and gas as a propellant. Twelve of the gas cells were filled with a propellant gas instead of lifting gas with a total volume of 30,000 cubic metres, enough for approximately 100 flight hours. The fuel tank had a gasoline volume of 67 flight hours. Using both gasoline and Blau gas could give 118 hours cruise.

Water as ballast

Dew and rainfall on the hull

In the airships → LZ 127 Graf Zeppelin and LZ 129 Hindenburg rain gutters were attached to the trunk to collect rainwater to fill the ballast water tanks during the trip. However, this procedure is weather dependent and is therefore not reliable as a standalone measure.

Water from the ground

Captain Ernst A. Lehmann described how during World War I Zeppelins would land on the sea and pick up temporary ballast water.[2] In 1921 the airships LZ 120 "Bodensee" and LZ 121 "Nordstern" tested the possibillity on Lake Constance to use lake water to create ballast. These attempts, however, showed no satisfactory results.

Silica-gel method

The silica gel method was tested on the LZ 129 to extract water from the humid air to increase weight. The project was terminated.

Water from fuel combustion

The most promising procedure for ballast extraction during the journey is condensation of exhaust gasses from the engines which consist mainly of water (steam) and carbon dioxide. The main factors affecting gainable water are the hydrogen content of the fuel and humidity. The necessary exhaust gas coolers for this method had repeatedly problems with corrosion in the early years.

The first trials on the DELAG -Zeppelin LZ 13 "Hansa" (1912-1916) were conducted by Wilhelm Maybach. The trials were not satisfactory, resulting in an abandoned project.

The condensors of the Macon's water recovery system appear as dark vertical strips above each engine. The Akron and → LZ 130 Graf Zeppelin had similar systems.

The United States Navy reports the USS Shenandoah (ZR-1) (1923-25) , a helium-filled rigid airship, as the first airship with ballast water from the condensation of exhaust gas. The LZ 126/ZR-3 USS Los Angeles was refitted with helium as a lifting gas after arrival in the U.S. Exhaust gas coolers were used to prevent jettisoning of the costly helium.

Lifting gas temperature

Changes in the lifting gas temperature in relation to the surrounding air have an effect on the buoyancy balance: higher temperatures increase buoyancy; lower temperatures descrease buoyancy. Artificially changing the lifting gas temperature requires constant work as the gas is barely thermally isolated from the surrounding air. However, it was common to make use of natural differences in temperature such as thermal updrafts and clouds.

Preheated lifting gas

Preheated lifting gas was tested to offset the higher weight of the Zeppelin. One variation tested on the LZ 127 Graf Zeppelin was to blow heated air on the lifting gas storage cells with the aim to gain buoyancy for launch.

See also

- Aerostat
- Blimp

External links

- Patentschrift zum Auftreibsausgleich durch Kondensation und Verdampfung von Wasserdampf [3] (German)

References

[1] Walrus (http://www.aerosml.com/redherring.asp)
[2] Lehmann, Ernst A.; Mingos, Howard. The Zeppelins. The Development of the Airship, with the Story of the Zepplins Air Raids in the World War. Chapter VI THE NORTH SEA PATROL -- THE ZEPPELINS AT JUTLAND (http://www.hydrogencommerce.com/zepplins/zeppelin6.htm) "A sea anchor is cast out and ballast tanks in the cars, which are almost as seaworthy as boats, are filled with water"
[3] http://publikationen.dpma.de/DPMApublikationen/pdf_any_all.do?hitlistCurrent=2&docId=DE10229378A1&docDate=22.01.2004&hitlistAll=2&id=7656636

LZ 130 Graf Zeppelin

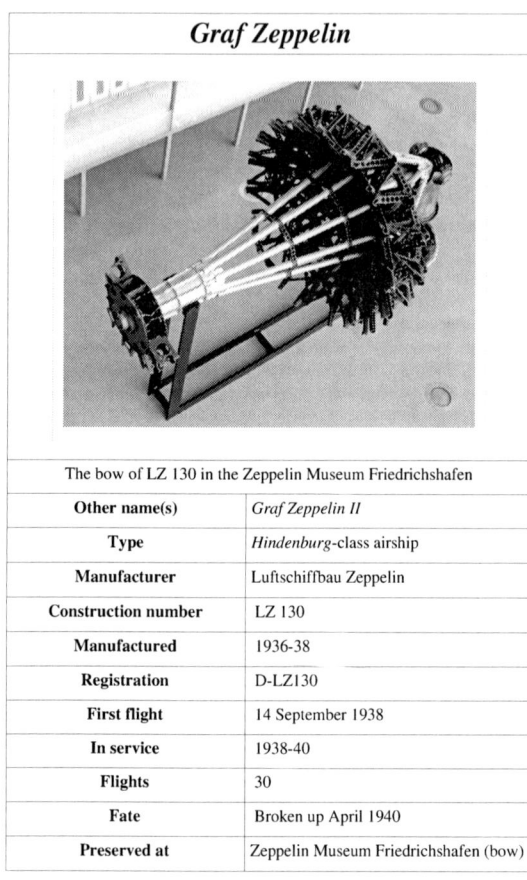

Graf Zeppelin

The bow of LZ 130 in the Zeppelin Museum Friedrichshafen

Other name(s)	*Graf Zeppelin II*
Type	*Hindenburg*-class airship
Manufacturer	Luftschiffbau Zeppelin
Construction number	LZ 130
Manufactured	1936-38
Registration	D-LZ130
First flight	14 September 1938
In service	1938-40
Flights	30
Fate	Broken up April 1940
Preserved at	Zeppelin Museum Friedrichshafen (bow)

The *Graf Zeppelin II* (Deutsche Luftschiff Zeppelin #130; Registration: **D-LZ 130**) was the last of the great German rigid airships built by the Zeppelin Luftschiffbau during the period between the World Wars, the second and final ship of the *Hindenburg* class. She was the second ship to carry the name "Graf Zeppelin" (after the → LZ 127), and thus she is often referred to as *Graf Zeppelin II*.

Design and development

The design of LZ-130 incorporated a few improvements over the design of the *Hindenburg*. Most visibly, the engine pods were completely redesigned, using diesel engines powering tractor propellers. The engines had a water recovery system which captured the exhaust of the engines to minimize weight lost during flight. The passenger decks were also completely redesigned; the restaurant was moved to the middle of the quarters and the promenade windows were half a panel lower. The 16 gas cells were lightened and one was made of lightweight silk instead of cotton. There were also small redesigns done to numerous parts of the airship, such as the gas vent hoods, gondola windows and the landing wheel installation. Additionally, the doping compound for the outer fabric covering was also changed, bronze and graphite were added to prevent flammability and also improved the outer covering's electrical conductivity. With these improvements, LZ-130 can be regarded as the most technologically advanced rigid airship ever flown.

The *Graf Zeppelin II* was originally designed to use hydrogen as lifting gas. After the *Hindenburg* disaster, however, → Hugo Eckener vowed never to use hydrogen in a passenger airship again. Instead, he planned to use helium (which had also originally been planned as the lifting gas for the *Hindenburg*). The only source of helium in large enough quantities was in the United States, so Eckener went to Washington, D.C. to lobby for helium for his airships. He visited President Roosevelt himself, who promised to supply helium, but only for peaceful purposes. After the annexation of Austria in March 1938, U.S. Secretary of the Interior Harold Ickes refused to supply helium, and the *Graf Zeppelin II* was ultimately inflated with hydrogen. It has been suggested that the use of helium was ruled out on financial grounds.

Construction timeline

23 June 1936 - The keel of the airship was laid and the main rings were fastened onto the roof of the hangar.

14 February 1937 - The nose cone was installed. In the same month, the fabric was also applied over the framework.

6 May 1937 - The *LZ 129 Hindenburg* bursts into flames and crashes while landing at Lakehurst, NJ, killing 35 out of 97 people on board and one member of the ground crew.

15 August 1938 - Inflation began on gas cells.

20 August 1938 - Engines and electrical connections are tested.

22 August 1938 - The radio communication system is tested.

14 September 1938 the ship was christened and flew the first time. Unlike the christening of the *Hindenburg*, only Zeppelin Company officials and Hermann Göring were present; no other government representatives came to the christening to congratulate Eckener. The speech held Dr. Eckener.

14 November 1938 - By the time the *Graf Zeppelin II* was completed, it was obvious that the ship would never serve its intended purpose as a passenger liner; the lack of a supply of inert helium was one cause. The Reich Air Ministry permitted the *Graf Zeppelin* to fly for one year until 1 September 1939 "without any transportation of passengers and outside from tropical areas".

Operational history

In total, the Graf Zeppelin made thirty flights:[1]

Flights 1 to 7

1. 14 September 1938 - The maiden voyage took place immediately after the christening of the ship under the command of Dr. Hugo Eckener. The ship took off from Friedrichshafen at 7:50 with 74 people mainly Air Ministry, and Zeppelin Company officials on board. Also onboard were the builders, technicians and engineers of the airship. The engines were only started after the airship reached a height of approximately 100 m. The *Graf Zeppelin* flew across Munich, Augsburg and Ulm and returned the Friedrichshafen at 1:30 PM, travelling a total of 925 kilometres. Hugo Eckener described the trip as "satisfying" and "successful."[1]

2. 17 September - 18 September 1938 - The second trip was a 26-hour test trip under the command of Dr. Hugo Eckener and Captain Hans von Schiller with a total of 85 persons on board. It started at 8:08 AM on 17 September 1938. The morning was spent over the Bodensee with different measurements. At noon the ship flew north towards Stuttgart at 12:15 and Frankfurt am Main at 13:15, and then towards Eisenach and Eisleben. Towards evening Berlin was reached. After many circuits at low altitude the Graf started towards Hamburg. Over the outer-Elbe-estuary in the Wadden Sea further calibrations and tests were made. Afterwards it flew a direct course over Minden towards Frankfurt am Main and then towards Bodensee. There, the airship had to fly a large loop over Friedrichshafen, because the airfield lay in fog. At 10:17, LZ 130 landed after covering 2,388 km, and shortly before 11 o'clock was brought back into the Löwenthaler hangar.[1]

3. 22 September 1938 - The third trial flight; 8:13 - 19:30 1215-km loop over Munich and Vienna and back again.[1]

4. 25 September 1938 - Launch approx. 11:00 under Captain Hans von Schiller (duration approx. 7 h, 764 km, 40 crew members, 34 passengers and technicians). Tests at high altitude were made. Almost the whole trip took place at an altitude of about 2,000 m, without needing to valve much gas. Further atmospheric-electrical tests were made.[1]

5. 27 September 1938 - eleven hours of trip duration, on behalf of the Reich Air Ministry (RLM). At the airport and airship-port *Rhein-Main* a radio beacon was set up. The idea was to attempt a *Funkbeschickung* (a calibration of the direction-finding equipment). Hazy air hindered the attempts despite good weather conditions. The calibration did not succeed perfectly - these problems arose even at later attempts. There were also first successes with the *Ballastwassergewinnungsanlage* (a water recovery system to save ballast). Three and a half tonnes of ballast water could be saved and the engines ran quieter because of the sound-absorbing effect of the device.[1]

6 28 September 1938 - Further test flight on behalf of the RLM under Captain Sammt. Among other things, the test was intended to investigate whether electrostatic charges caused the Hindenburg disaster. Therefore it was especially flown during thunderstorms. Flights during normal weather conditions brought no useful results. The ship was flown into the stormfront slack (gas cells under-expanded), to prevent the over-pressure valves releasing hydrogen. The trip lasted nearly 26 hours; covering over 2,500 km. The ballast water recovery system fulfilled the engineers' expectations by producing about nine tons of water.[1]

7. 31 October 1938 launch around 2:15 under the command of Captain Sammt. This was simultaneously the last inspection flight and the transfer flight to *Flug- und Luftschiffhafen Frankfurt am Main* (the airship port at Frankfurt am Main). It landed after nearly 25 hours, covering over 2,100 km around 15:10. The airship and the crew were welcomed by *Gauleiter* Sprenger at the new home port. After this trip LZ 130 on 14 November 1938 received the *Luftschiff-Zulassungsschein* (airship registration document). Thus it was certified for air traffic and registered in the German *Luftfahrzeugrolle* (aircraft register), however with the restriction of no carriage of passengers.[1]

Flight 8 - *Sudetenlandfahrt*

8. "Sudetenlandfahrt" - This flight, also known as the *Sudetenduetsch Freiheitsfahrt 1938*, was made at the behest of the Reich Ministry for Public Enlightenment and Propaganda (*Reichsministerium für Volksaufklärung und Propaganda* or *Propagandaministerium*. After the popular vote resulted in a large majority for Hitler and the NSDAP many propaganda channels were used - including a Zeppelin flight over the *befreiten Gebiete* (liberated regions). On board were 62 crew members and 7 passengers, among them military officers. The launch occurred on 2 December 1938 shortly after 10 o'clock. Over Reichenberg (present-day Liberec), capital of Sudetenland, over which LZ 130 floated exactly at Hitler's visit, were thrown out small parachutes with swastika flags and handbills with the text "*Dein JA dem Führer!*" ("Your YES for the leader"). LZ 130's loudspeakers played music and National Socialist propaganda for the forthcoming December 4 elections. Afterwards LZ 130 flew to the Reichenberg airfield and dropped 663 kg of postally cacheted souvenir mails (see image above). Worsening weather hindered further flight, therefore after some time it was decided to turn back. After the ship left the Sudetenland, it came into low cloud and snow showers. It

Post card carried on the *Sudetendeutsche Freiheitsfahrt 1938*

started to ice up. Later, the propellers blew broken-off ice shards through the ship's outer envelope. However, the crew immediately repaired the damage. At 17:46 the Zeppelin landed without problem in gusty winds and was brought into the airship hangar.[1]

Flights 9 to 23

9. 1939-01-13 launched at 9:08, commanded by captain Sammt, different tests were performed. Duration: 7 hours and 523 km

10. 1939-04-13 Among other things, radio- and spy basket tests were performed. The trip lasted approximately 30 hours and covered nearly 2,700 km.

11. 1939-06-15 Duration: 28 hours; 2,800 km

12. and 13. *Meiningenfahrt* 1939-07-02; 18:40 landing at Meiningen airfield, flew back to Frankfurt am Main at 19:22.

14. and 15. *Leipzigfahrt* (Leipzig trip) 9 July 1939; among other things landing in Leipzig-Mockau airfield with post office delivery

16. *Nordseefahrt* (North Sea trip) launch: 1939-07-12 22:25

17. and 18. *Görlitzfahrt* (Görlitz trip) launch: 1939-08-16 00:34 under captain Sammt

19. 20., and **21.** *Bielefeld-Münster-Fahrt* (Bielefeld-Münster trip)

22. and 23. *Kasselfahrtt* (Kassel trip)

Flight 24 - *Spionagefahrt*

24. The *Spionagefahrt* ("espionage trip") of 2 to 4 August 1939, taking over 48 hours and covering 4.203 km, was the longest trip the LZ 130 made. The main goal was to secretly collect information on the English Chain Home radar system.[2] To do this the airship flew northwards close to the British east coast up to the Shetland Isles and back. On board were 45 crew and 28 measurement personnel. Lift off was on 1939-08-02 around 20:53,[1] and it overflew Hildesheim at 23:38, seen by very few people.[2]

The memoirs of Albert Sammt, *Mein Leben für den Zeppelin* (translation: "My life for the zeppelin") written by Dr. Ernst Breuning, describes this trip in chapter *Mit LZ 130 Graf Zeppelin auf Funkhorch- und Funkortungsfahr* (translation: "with the LZ 130 Graf Zeppelin on the radio-listening and radiolocation trip").[1]

These memoirs detailed the spying trip of 2 to 4 August 1939 when a radio-measuring spy basket was used. He flew the LZ 130 up Britain's east coat to the Shetland Isles and flew slowly back, stopping the engines at Aberdeen (pretending they had engine failure) in order to investigate strange antenna masts. As a free balloon they drifted westwards over the land and for the first time sighted and photographed the new Supermarine Spitfires, which circled the airship.[3]

On the evening of 4 August as they neared Frankfurt on their return from this trip they were warned on longwave radio that landing was not yet possible. They first suspected an aeroplane had crashed at the site, but on overflying saw nothing amiss. They turned and flew towards the Rhön Mountains and on asking, were informed "landing before dusk not possible". They decided to return to Frankfurt and speak directly with the *Landemannschaft* (landing team) using the *UKW* transmitter, so that the French wouldn't overhear and so that they could use Schwäbisch to speak to Beurle, the landing team leader.[3]

Beurle informed them they must not land yet because the English had lodged a diplomatic protest over their actions. Furthermore an English delegation was at the airfield, with agreement of the German government, to inspect the ship. They were under suspicion. Beurle told them to wait while they think of something.[3]

Shortly, the LZ 130 received the advice: hide all the measuring instruments in the ship; don't land at the usual well-lit landing-cross where a landing team is waiting, but land at the other end where the "real" landing team is waiting and will make itself known with light signals; after landing let the Breuning people out and let a *SA-Sturm* on as pretend-crew.

So, the English were waiting at the false landing place, and were told that for meteorological reasons the airship had to land at another part of the airfield. By the time the English crossed the airfield to the airship, the "real" crew was on a bus on their way to their hotel. The English searched the ship, found nothing suspicious, neither in the ship nor in the false SA-crew.[3]

Dr Breuning explained that the trip's results were negative, and not because the British radar was switched off, as Churchill wrote in his memoirs. The German General Martini used a strong, impulsive, broadband radio transmission for determining the "radio-weather", the best wavelengths to use for radio. These impulses severely disturbed the highly sensitive receivers in the 10-12 metre waveband. Dr. Ernst Breuning wrote that he repeatedly requested Martini to stop transmitting during the spy trips, to no avail. This made it impossible for the LZ 130 to investigate the very wavebands the British were using.[3]

Flights 25 to 30

25. and 26. *Würzburgfahrt* (Würzburg trip) 1939-08-05

27. and 28. *Egerfahrt* (Eger trip) 1939-08-13

29 and 30. The last trip, the so-called *Essen/Mülheim-Fahrt* (Essen/Mülheim trip), took place on 1939-08-20. The departure and destination was Frankfurt am Main with an intermediate stop at Essen/Mülheim Airport (IATA code: ESS), commanded by Albert Sammt. This trip (landing at 21:38) meant the end of large airship transport.[1]

Graf Zeppelin II in color

Along with the Hindenburg, which was photographed in construction and flight 1936 and its burning wreckage in 1937, the *Graf Zeppelin II* is the only zeppelin that has been filmed in color. Several color photographs of the airship survive[4], as well as color footage shot by Harold G. Dick of the ship over Friedrichshafen. The latter was shown in the 2001 documentary *Hindenburg Disaster: Probable Cause*, but was mistaken for colour footage of the Hindenburg.

The archives of the Zeppelin Museum Friedrichshafen also has a yearbook featuring color photographs of both airships taken by Captain Hans von Schiller. [5]

The end of the airships

In April 1940, Hermann Göring issued the order to scrap both *Graf Zeppelins* and the unfinished framework of LZ 131, since the metal was needed for other aircraft. By April 27, work crews had finished cutting up the airships. On May 6, the enormous airship hangars in Frankfurt were leveled by explosives, three years to the day after the destruction of the *Hindenburg*.

Specifications

General characteristics

- **Crew:** ca. 40
- **Capacity:** ca. 40 passengers
- **Length:** 244 m (803 ft 10 in)
- **Diameter:** 41.2 m (135 ft 0 in)
- **Volume:** 200,000 m³ (7,100,000 ft³)
- **Useful lift:** 10,000 kg (22,000 lb)
- **Powerplant:** 4 × Daimler-Benz DB 602 16-cylinder diesel, 735 kW (985 hp) each

Performance
- **Maximum speed:** 131 km/h (81 mph)

See also
- → Buoyancy compensator (aviation)

Related lists
- → List of Zeppelins

References
[1] Editors of German wikipedia article http://de.wikipedia.org/wiki/LZ_130, freely translated
[2] Schütz, Michael. Zeppeline über Hildesheim (http://www.stadtarchiv-hildesheim.de/publikationen/dok_19_zeppeline.htm), Hildesheim city archive. Last accessed 2008-08-02
[3] Sammt 1988
[4] Andreas Krug. www.luftschiff.de Photos (http://www.luftschiff.de/1_luftschiffe/lz130/1_130.htm), last accessed 2008-07-01
[5] http://www.airshipmodeler.com/forums/showthread.php?t=556

- Sammt, Albert. 1988. *Mein Leben für den Zeppelin*, Verlag Pestalozzi Kinderdorf Wahlwies 1988, ISBN 3-921583-02-0 - pages 167-168 (http://www.luftschiffharry.de/doku/LZ_130_Spionagefahrt.pdf) extract covering LZ 130's spying trip from 2 to 4 August 1939, (German) (pdf)

External links
- eZEP.de (http://www.ezep.de/index.html) — The webportal for Zeppelin mail and airship memorabilia
- Zeppelin Study Group (http://www.ezep.de/zsg/zsg.html) — Research group for airship memorabilia and Zeppelin mail
- GRAF ZEPPELIN - MAIDEN FLIGHT 19/09/1938 (http://www.britishpathe.com/thumbnails.php?id=31047&searchword=Graf Zeppelin&searchword=Graf Zeppelin) British Pathe Free Preview of maiden flight, Film ID: 981.27

List of Zeppelins

This is a complete **list of Zeppelins** constructed by the original German Zeppelin companies from 1900 until 1938. Other types of rigid → airships that are also sometimes referred to as zeppelins are not included.

The Zeppelin companies based in Friedrichshafen, Germany, numbered their aircraft *LZ1/2/*..., with *LZ* standing for "Luftschiff [airship] Zeppelin". Additionally, crafts used for civilian purposes usually got a name, while military airships, on the other hand, were given "tactical numbering":

- The *German Army* called its first Zeppelins *Z I/II/ ... /XI/XII*. During World War I they switched to using the *LZ* numbers, later adding 30 to obscure the total production.
- The *German Navy* Zeppelins were labelled *L 1/2/* ....

Since 1997, airships of the new type Zeppelin NT have been flying. They are not included here, as they are not Zeppelins in the traditional sense.

Zeppelins finished before World War I

Production number	Name / tactical numbering	Usage	First flight	Remarks	Image
LZ1		prototype	July 2, 1900 (L)	three flights, beat speed record set by La France, dismantled 1901 after lack of shareholder interest[1]	
LZ2		experimental	January 17, 1906	In 1905-11-30 never lifted off from lake; second attempt took flight but damaged beyond repair after emergency landing[1]	
LZ3	Z I	experimental; military	October 9, 1906[1]	flew for 2 hours in 1906-10-09 and in 1906-10-10, flew for 8 hours in 1907;[1] as part of LZ4's contract sold to the German Army in 1908 after refitting; used as a school ship; decommissioned in 1913 (D)	
LZ4		military (intended)	June 20, 1908	part of contract including LZ3; 12 hour flight on 1908-07-01; attempted contractual 24 hour endurance flight on 1908-08-04, landed near Echterdingen after 12 hours to repair an engine but destroyed when wind broke its moorings;[1] ; see Zeppelin#The First Generations	
LZ5	Z II	experimental; military	May 26, 1909	stranded near Weilburg in 1910 during a storm (D)	
LZ6		experimental; civilian (DELAG)	August 25, 1909 (L)	first experiments with wireless communication; first *DELAG* craft (see Zeppelin); accidentally destroyed in its hangar in Baden-Oos in 1910 (D)	
LZ7	"Deutschland"	civilian (DELAG)	June 19, 1910	damaged beyond repair in an accident above the Teutoburg Forest on June 28, 1910 (D)	
LZ8	Ersatz "Deutschland II"	civilian (DELAG)	March 30, 1911	pushed to the wall of its hangar by strong wind and damaged beyond repair on May 16, 1911 (D)	
LZ9	Ersatz Z II	military	October 2, 1911 (L)	decommissioned August 1, 1914 (D)	
LZ10	"Schwaben"	civilian (DELAG)	June 26, 1911 (D)	transported 4354 passengers in 224 flights, traveling 27,321 km; destroyed June 28, 1912 in accident on the airfield in Düsseldorf (D)	

List of Zeppelins

LZ11	"Viktoria Luise"	civilian (DELAG); later military	February 19, 1912	transported 9783 passengers in 489 flights, traveling 54,312 km; taken over as school ship by German military upon outbreak of World War I; broke apart while being *hauled in* (i.e. put into its hangar) on October 1, 1915[2] (D)	
LZ12	Z III	military	April 25, 1912	decommissioned August 1, 1914 (D)	
LZ13	"Hansa"	civilian (DELAG); later military	July 30, 1912	traveled 44,437 km in 399 flights; first regular flight outside Germany (commanded by Count Zeppelin on first visit to Denmark and Sweden in 1912-09-19);[3] taken over by German military upon outbreak of World War I; decommissioned in summer 1916 (D)	
LZ14	L 1	military	October 7, 1912 (L)	pushed down into the North Sea in a thunderstorm on September 9, 1913, drowning 14 crew members. *This was the first Zeppelin incident in which fatalities occurred* (D)	
LZ15	Ersatz Z I	military	January 16, 1913	destroyed in a forced landing on March 19, 1913 (D)	
LZ16	Z IV	military	March 14, 1913	accidentally crossed French border on April 3, 1913 in misty weather and was kept in Lunéville for one day. Performed some reconnaissance missions in World War I and attempted bombing of Warsaw and Lyck. Used as a school ship from 1915; decommissioned in autumn of 1916 (D) (Z IV crew [4] showing their Iron Crosses)	
LZ17	"Sachsen"	civilian; later military	May 3, 1913	transported 9837 passengers in 419 flights, traveling 39,919 km; taken over by German military upon outbreak of World War I in 1914; this was Captain Lehmann's first command; it had bomb racks and bomb drop station fitted, together with an improved radio room, machine guns in the cars below and a gunners nest on top of the tail;[5] In its first attack on Antwerp it carried 1800 pounds (820 kg) of bombs and spent 12 hours in the air.[6] Decommissioned in autumn of 1916 (D)	
LZ18	L 2	military	September 9, 1913	destroyed by an exploding engine on October 17, 1913 during a test flight; the entire crew was killed. (D)	
LZ19	Second Ersatz Z I	military	June 6, 1913	damaged beyond repair in a thunderstorm on June 13, 1914 (D)	
LZ20	Z V	military	July 8, 1913	used in World War I for reconnaissance missions in western Poland; forced landing after an attack on Mława during the Battle of Tannenberg; crew captured by enemy cavalry while trying to burn down the ship. (D)	
LZ21	Z VI	military	November 10, 1913	In World War I mainly used in Belgium as a bomber; during a bombing raid of Liège dropping artillery shells instead of bombs, the ship's overweightness kept it at low altitude so that the bullets and shrapnel from defending fire penetrated the hull. The ship limped back to Cologne but had to be set down near Bonn in a forest, completely wrecking it, on August 6, 1914.[5]	

List of Zeppelins

LZ22	Z VII	military	January 8, 1914	Limited to a flight ceiling around one mile. On August 21, 1914 sent to find the retreating French Army around the Vosges mountains in Alsace, and dropped bombs on the camps. After passing through clouds found itself low, right above the main army whose infantry fire penetrated many gas cells. The ship leaking heavily, the crew forced it down near St. Quirin, Lorraine.[5]	
LZ23	Z VIII	military	May 11, 1914	same orders as *Z VII* on August 21, 1914; engaged French army while a few hundred feet up and according to Lehmann received "thousands of bullets and shell splinters"; this forced it to drift and a forced landing in no man's land near Bandonvillers; the crew destroyed all documents and tried to burn the wreck but so little gas remained it would not burn; French Cavalry arrive and a gunfight ensues, the German crew retreating;[5] captured and plundered by French army	
LZ24	L 3	military	May 11, 1914	24 reconnaissance missions over the North Sea; participated in the first raid of England on January 19, 1915; released by its crew after a forced landing (due to engine failure compounded with strong headwind and insufficient fuel to reach Germany) in Denmark on February 17, 1915. The wind was so strong it blew the now unmanned but still running airship out across the sea.[7]	
LZ25	Z IX	military	July 13, 1914	used for reconnaissance missions and bombings in northern France; destroyed by English bomber aeroplane which dropped a bomb through the hangar roof in Düsseldorf on October 8, 1914.[6] The bomber was a single-seat Sopwith Tabloid flown by Flt Lt Reginald Marix, RNAS (later Air Vice Marshal); he had flown from Antwerp and the raid was the first strategic bombing raid by an airplane.[8]	

Key:

- D indicates translated summary from a sighted version from [9]
- L indicates data from Lueger 1904.[10]

Zeppelins constructed during World War I

Usage: military

Production number	Tactical numbering	First flight	Remarks
LZ26	Z XII (Z 12)	December 14, 1914	11 attacks in northern France and at the eastern front, dropping 20,000 kg of bombs; By the summer of 1915 the LZ 12 had dropped around 9 tons of bombs on the trunk railway line between Warsaw and Petrograd and the stations at Malkin and Bialystok; one flight carried a load of 3 tons.[11] Decommissioned on August 8, 1917.
LZ27	L 4	August 18, 1914	11 reconnaissance missions over the North Sea; participated in the first raid of England on January 20, 1915. Forced landing in Blavandshuk on February 17, 1915 due to a storm; the crew was taken captive, with four members reported missing in action. Flight Magazine 1916 reports that it was probably *L 3* that was stranded at Ebsjerg on that day, with the crew of 16 being interned.[12]
LZ28	L 5	September 22, 1914	47 reconnaissance missions over North and Baltic Sea; proved especially useful in discovering enemy mines; two attack missions, dropping 700 kg bombs; damaged beyond repair by Russian air defense on August 7, 1915
LZ29	Z X	October 13, 1914	Two attacks on Calais and Paris, dropping 1,800 kg of bombs; on way back damaged by enemy fire and dismantled after forced landing in St. Quirin

LZ30	Z XI	November 15, 1914	Used for raids on Warsaw, Grodno and other targets near the eastern front. Destroyed in an accident on May 20, 1915
LZ31	L 6	November 3, 1914	Prominent role in repelling a British Navy attack on German coast on December 25, 1914; 36 reconnaissance missions around North Sea, including marking of mine fields; one successful raid on England, dropping 700 kg of bombs. Took fire during refilling of gas in its hall at Fuhlsbüttel and burnt down together with *L 9* on September 16, 1916.
LZ32	L 7	November 20, 1914	77 reconnaissance missions over the North Sea; several unsuccessful attempts to attack English coast. Brought down by British cruiser fire from HMS *Phaeton* and *Galatea* and destroyed by the submarine HMS *E31* on May 4, 1916
LZ33	L 8	December 17, 1914	Used for reconnaissance missions along the western front. Flight Magazine 1916 lists it as "Damaged by British aviator", it wrecked south of Ostend at Tirlemont on 4 March 1915 with the crew of 21 killed.[12]
LZ34		January 6, 1915	Two raids at the eastern front, dropping 1110 kg bombs; heavily damaged by enemy fire on June 21, 1915, burnt down following forced landing near Insterburg.
LZ35		January 11, 1915	Two raids on Paris and Poperinghe (Belgium), dropping 2420 kg bombs; forced landing near Aeltre (Belgium) due to heavy damage by enemy fire, then destroyed by a storm.
LZ36	L 9	8 March 1915	74 reconnaissance missions in the North Sea; four raids on England dropping 5683 kg bombs; several attacks on British submarines. Burnt out in its hangar on September 16, 1916 together with *L 6*.
LZ37		March 4, 1915	Flight Magazine 1916 lists LZ 37 as "Destroyed in shed by British aviators" on 7 June 1915 at Evere.[12] Brought down by Flt Sub-Lt R Warneford, 1 Sqdn RNAS, flying a Morane-Saulnier Type L, during its first raid on Calais on 7 June 1915. Warneford was awarded a Victoria Cross for his actions.[13]
LZ38		April 3, 1915	Achieved first bombing raid on London on May 31, 1915 killing 7 and injuring 35 people (with material damage assessed at £18,596), five successful raids on Harwich, Ramsgate, Southend (twice) and London, dropping 8360 kg bombs. Flight Magazine 1916 listed LZ 38 as "destroyed in mid-air by British aviator" at Ghent on 7 June 1915.[12]
LZ39	LZ39	April 24, 1915	Three raids at the western, later two at the eastern front, dropping 4184 kg bombs in total. On December 17, 1915, captained by Dr. Lempertz, during an attack on Rovno LZ-39 was hit several times by artillery shrapnel. All rear gas cells were punctured and the front engine car was hit and later fell off. The crew abandoned the now-stressed control cabin, dropped ballast and shifted loads to rebalance the ship and used an emergency control station in the rear to limp back to Germany. Upon forced landing the ship collapsed because material and a supply of gas needed to refill the cells was not available.[14]
LZ40	L 10	May 13, 1915	8 reconnaissance missions around the North Sea; 5 attacks on England dropping 9900 kg bombs, including the first raid on London on August 17–18 1915 during which Leyton was bombed causing ten deaths and injuring 48 people. Destroyed in a thunderstorm on September 3, 1915 near Cuxhaven
LZ41	L 11	June 7, 1915	31 reconnaissance missions, notably during the Battle of Jutland; 12 raids on England dropping 15,543 kg bombs. Several of the L11 crew transferred to the ill-fated L48 (LZ95).[15] Decommissioned on April 25, 1916
LZ42	LZ72	June 15, 1915	Only used as a school ship, as skeleton metal was of poor quality; decommissioned in February 1917
LZ43	L 12	June 21, 1915	5 reconnaissance missions; towed back to Ostend after taking heavy damage in a raid on London, Harwich and the Humber region on August 10, 1915 but burned out during subsequent disassembly.
LZ44	LZ74	July 8, 1915	Two attacks on England dropping 3500 kg bombs; dismantled after it crashed into a mountain in misty weather on October 8, 1915.
LZ45	L 13	July 23, 1915	45 reconnaissance missions; 15 attacks on England dropping 20,667 kg bombs; decommissioned on April 25, 1917
LZ46	L 14	August 9, 1915	Most successful German Navy airship; 42 reconnaissance missions; 17 attacks on England dropping 22,045 kg bombs; taken out of service during 1917 and 1918. Destroyed by its crew on June 23, 1919.

List of Zeppelins

LZ47	LZ77	August 24, 1915	6 attacks on England and France dropping 12,610 kg bombs. Destroyed by enemy fire on February 21, 1916 in the Battle of Verdun, killing the crew of 15.[12] Reports at the time indicated LZ 77 had searchlights, eight machine guns, two so-called 'revolver' guns in the top lookout post, was accompanied by fixed-wing aircraft and at least one other Zeppelin and had orders to bomb the nearby railway lines.[16][17]
LZ48	L 15	September 9, 1915	8 reconnaissance missions; 3 attacks on England dropping 5780 kg bombs. Damaged by ground fire from Dartford AA battery during a raid on London on April 1, 1916, it was stranded at Kentish Knock Deep in the Thames estuary, the crew of 18 surrendered before the craft sank.[12]
LZ49	LZ79	August 2, 1915	Dropped 4440 kg in two attacks on Brest-Litovsk and Kovel and one attack on Paris on January 30, 1916; thereby hit by French fire and damaged beyond repair in forced landing near Ath.
LZ50	L 16	September 23, 1915	44 reconnaissance missions; 12 attacks on England dropping 18,048 kg bombs; delivered supplies to German isles in winter 1916. Damaged beyond repair in a forced landing near Brunsbüttel on October 19, 1917.
LZ51	LZ81	October 7, 1915	Used at the South-Eastern and the Western Front; transported a diplomatic commission over enemy Serbia on November 9, 1915; one attack on Étaples (France) and two attacks on Bucharest, dropping 4513 kg bombs in total; stranded near Turnovo (Bulgaria) on September 27, 1916. (Luftschifferalltag [18] Christmas celebration table under the Z 81 in its hangar)
LZ52	L 18	November 3, 1915	Destroyed in shed fire at Tondern on 17 November 1915[12]
LZ53	L 17	October 20, 1915	27 reconnaissance missions; 9 attacks on England dropping 10,724 kg bombs. Destroyed in its hangar on December 28, 1916 when *LZ69 "L 24"* broke its back and took fire across the hall's entrance.
LZ54	L 19	November 27, 1915	It raided England on 31 January 1916, dropping 1600 kg bombs. On 21 February 1916 after a raid on England[12] with three engines failing, it came under Dutch fire and sank in the North Sea, drowning all crew members as nearby English fishing trawler "King Stephen" refused any help to them.[19] [Kapitan-Leutnant Loewe]
LZ55	LZ85	September 12, 1915	6 attacks dropping 14,200 kg on Dünaburg (Latvia), Minsk, the railroads of Riga,[14] and Saloniki (three times); damaged by fire from Battleship HMS *Agamemnon* on May 5, 1916, it was stranded in the Wardar marshes
LZ56	LZ86	October 10, 1915	7 attacks dropping 14,800 kg bombs along the Eastern and South-Eastern front; crashed on September 3, 1916 when the fore and aft nacelle broke away from the ship's hull after a raid.
LZ57	LZ87	December 6, 1915	2 attacks on Ramsgate and Margate dropping 3000 kg bombs; in July 1916 handed to the German Navy; 16 reconnaissance missions around the Baltic Sea; later used as a school ship. Decommissioned in July 1917.
LZ58	LZ88/L 25	November 14, 1915	14 reconnaissance missions; 3 attacks dropping 4249 kg bombs along the Western Front; in January 1917 handed to the German Navy who used it for experimenting. Decommissioned in September 1917.

LZ59	L 20	November 21, 1915	6 reconnaissance missions; 2 attacks on England dropping 2864 kg bombs; ran out of fuel after raiding Scotland on 3 May 1916, drifted and stranded near Stavanger (Norway). The crew destroyed the airship. 16 were captured, 3 died.[12] Kapitänleutnant Stabbert escaped six months later.
LZ60	LZ90	January 1, 1916	4 attacks on Bar-le-Duc, Norwich, London and Etaples, dropping 8860 kg bombs; on November 7, 1916 broke loose in the direction of the North Sea in a storm and never seen again.
LZ61	L 21	January 10, 1916	17 reconnaissance missions; 10 attacks on England dropping 14,442 kg bombs; intercepted and destroyed by English fighter pilot Flt-Lt Egbert Cadbury firing phosphor rounds off Lowestoft on November 28, 1916.
LZ62	L 30	May 28, 1916	First of the "Super-Zeppelin" Class, it had a volume of 55,200m³. 10 raids on England dropping 23,305 kg bombs (however causing limited damage due to poor sight); 31 reconnaissance missions above the North and Baltic Sea and at the Eastern Front; retired on November 17, 1917 and laided up at Seerappen. In 1920 ordered to be transferred to Belgium in the context of war reparations, where it was disassembled. Some components, including an engine car, are preserved at the Royal Army and Military History Museum, Brussels.
LZ63	LZ93	February 23, 1916	Three attacks on Dunkirk, Mardick and Harwich, dropping 3240 kg bombs. Decommissioned in 1917.
LZ64	L 22	March 3, 1916	30 reconnaissance missions; 8 attacks on England, dropping 9215 kg bombs; destroyed by British Curtis H12 Flying Boat flown by RNAS Flight Commander Robert Leckie (later Air Vice Marshal) near Terschelling on May 14, 1917 during a reconnaissance mission.[20] (Leckie was also credited in the downing on LZ112/L70)
LZ65	LZ95	February 1, 1916	Destroyed by French anti-aircraft fire on February 21, 1915 during an attempted attack on Vitry-le-François.
LZ66	L 23	April 8, 1916	51 reconnaissance missions; 3 attacks on England dropping a total of 5,254 kg bombs; destroyed on August 21, 1917 by 2/Lt Bernard A Smart flying a Sopwith Pup launched from a platofrm on the cruiser HMS *Yarmouth*.[21] Smart later led the Tondern raid which destroyed L54 & L60.
LZ67	LZ97	April 4, 1916	4 attacks on London (twice), Boulogne and, later, Bucharest, dropping 5760 kg bombs, plus several unsuccessful flights in bad weather. Decommissioned on July 5, 1917.
LZ68	LZ98	April 28, 1916	One attack on London dropping 1513 kg bombs, plus several flights aborted due to bad weather; handed to the German Navy in November 1916; 15 reconnaissance missions around the Baltic Sea. Decommissioned in August 1917.
LZ69	L 24	May 20, 1916	19 reconnaissance missions around the North Sea; 4 raids on England dropping 8510 kg bombs; crashed into a wall while being "stabled" on December 28, 1916 and burned out together with *LZ53 "L 17"*.
LZ70			*Not realized*
LZ71	LZ101	June 29, 1916	Stationed in Yambol (Bulgaria); 7 attacks dropping 11,934 kg bombs on Bucharest, Ciulnița, Fetești, Galați, Odessa, Mytilene, Iași and Mudros. Disassembled in September 1917.

List of Zeppelins

LZ72	L 31	July 12, 1916	*LZ72 or LZ74* One important reconnaissance mission in fleet operation against Sunderland; 6 attacks on England dropping 19,411 kg bombs; with L 32, L 33 and L 34 part of Zeppelin raid on night of 1916-09-23;[22] intercepted and destroyed by British fighter pilot Lt V Tempest on October 2, 1916 near Potters Bar, North of London, while commanded by the leading airship commander of the time, Kapitän Leutnant Heinrich Mathy, who perished with his entire crew, after jumping from the flaming Zeppelin and perishing some time after impact with the ground.
LZ73	LZ103	August 23, 1916	One successful attack on Calais dropping 1530 kg bombs (several other attacks being cancelled or aborted due to poor weather); decommissioned in August 1917
LZ74	L 32	August 4, 1916	One important reconnaissance mission in fleet operation against Sunderland; three attacks on England dropping 6860 kg bombs; commanded by Kapitan-Leutnant Werner Petersen, with L 31, L 33 and L 34 part of Zeppelin raid on night of 1916-09-23; intercepted and destroyed by 39 Squadron British fighter pilot 2/Lt Frederick Sowrey in a BE2c on September 24, 1916 near Great Burstead, Essex, all the crew dying.[22] The crew's bodies were buried at Great Burstead, then in 1966 exhumed and reburied at Cannock Chase.[22]
LZ75	L 37	November 9, 1916	17 reconnaissance missions around the North and Baltic Sea and England; 4 raids dropping 6450 kg bombs; retired on December 24, 1917; transferred to Japan in 1920 (disassembled)
LZ76	L 33	August 30, 1916	Part of the Zeppelin group that bombed London and surrounding counties (L31, L32, L33 and L34); during its first mission, in which 3200 kg bombs had been dropped, after an anti-aircraft shell seriously damaged it, commander Kapitan-Leutnant Alois Bocker turned over Essex and was attacked by 39 Home Defence Squadron night fighters from Hainault Farm and hit several times (credit for disabling given to B.E.2c No. 4544), but even after dropping guns and equipment Bocker decided it would not make it back across the North Sea, forced landing in Little Wigborough, Essex 24 September, 1916 with no fatalities,[22] the crew were only partly successful in burning the hull, and British engineers examined the skeleton and later used the plans as a basis for the construction of airships *R33* and *R34*
LZ77	LZ107	October 16, 1916	One attack on Boulogne, France, dropping 1440 kg bombs (several other raids being cancelled or aborted). Decommissioned in July 1917.
LZ78	L 34	September 22, 1916	Three reconnaissance missions; two attacks on England dropping 3890 kg bombs; intercepted and destroyed by British fighter pilot 2/Lt Ian Pyott in BE2c 2738 off Hartlepool on November 28, 1916.*Pyott was so close that his face was scorched*
LZ79	L 41	January 15, 1917	15 reconnaissance missions around the North Sea; four attacks on England dropping 6567 kg bombs; used as a school ship from December 11, 1917 on. Destroyed by its crew on June 23, 1919.
LZ80	L 35	October 20, 1916	13 reconnaissance missions around the North and Baltic Sea; three attacks on England dropping 4284 kg bombs; decommissioned in September 1918.
LZ81	LZ111	December 20, 1916	Not used in the German Army and transferred to Navy in May 1917; 7 reconnaissance missions around the Baltic Sea. Decommissioned on August 10, 1917.
LZ82	L 36	November 1, 1916	20 flights around the North Sea and England, including four reconnaissance missions; damaged during landing in fog at Rehben-an-der-Aller on February 7, 1917 and decommissioned.
LZ83	LZ113	February 22, 1917	15 reconnaissance missions around the Eastern Front and the Baltic Sea; three attacks dropping 6000 kg bombs. In 1920 ordered to be transferred to France in the context of war reparations.
LZ84	L 38	November 22, 1916	Damaged beyond repair in a forced landing (due to heavy snowfall) during an attempted raid on Reval and Saint Petersburg on December 29, 1916

LZ85	L 45	April 12, 1917	12 reconnaissance missions around the North Sea; 3 attacks on England dropping 4700 kg bombs. Ran out of fuel on October 20, 1917; destroyed in forced landing near Sisteron, France, the crew being taken captive.
LZ86	L 39	December 11, 1916	Two reconnaissance missions around the North Sea; one attack on England dropping 300 kg bombs, and on return destroyed by French flak fire near Compiègne on March 17, 1917.
LZ87	L 47	May 11, 1917	18 reconnaissance missions and three attacks dropping 3240 kg bombs around the North Sea and England. On January 5, 1918, a giant explosion in the air base in Ahlhorn destroyed four Zeppelins (including *L 47*) and one non-Zeppelin-type airship, stabled in three adjacent hangars. This is supposed to have been an accident, though sabotage could not be ruled out.
LZ88	L 40	January 3, 1917	6 reconnaissance missions; 2 attacks on England, dropping 3105 kg bombs (large parts of which missed their targets). Damaged beyond repair in a failed landing on June 16, 1917 in Nordholz.
LZ89	L 50	June 9, 1917	5 reconnaissance missions around the North Sea; two attacks on England dropping 4135 kg bombs. Ran out of fuel on October 20, 1917 and was driven to the Mediterranean Sea after a forced landing near Dammartin, France.
LZ90	LZ120	January 31, 1917	17 reconnaissance missions and 3 attacks dropping 11,250 kg bombs around the Eastern Front and the Baltic Sea. Retired on October 8, 1917; in 1920 ordered to be transferred to Italy in the context of war reparations, where it broke apart one year later while gas was removed.
LZ91	L 42	February 21, 1917	First of the "Height-Climber" class, which had a lightened structure to improve altitude. The strength of the structure was therefore compromised, which proved disastrous when unwittingly copied, as with the British *R38 (ZR-2)*, and USS *Shenandoah*. 20 reconnaissance missions; 4 attacks on England dropping 6030 kg bombs; used as a school ship from June 6, 1918 on. Destroyed by its crew on June 23, 1919.
LZ92	L 43	March 6, 1917	6 reconnaissance missions; one attack on English docks, dropping 1850 kg bombs. Shot down by British fighter aircraft on June 14, 1917 during reconnaissance mission.
LZ93	L 44	April 1, 1917	8 reconnaissance missions; 4 attacks on England and British Royal Navy units. Driven south to France by a heavy storm, it was shot down over Lunéville on October 20, 1917.
LZ94	L 46	April 24, 1917	19 reconnaissance missions around the North Sea; 3 raids on England dropping 5700 kg bombs. Destroyed in the Ahlhorn explosion (see *LZ87 "L 47"*).
LZ95	L 48	May 22, 1917	Several of the L 11 crew transferred to the L 48;[15] one reconnaissance mission successful. As part of an attempted attack on London with 3 others became lost and was then intercepted and destroyed by British fighters over sea near Great Yarmouth on 17 June 1917 crashing near Leiston. Three survivors; crew buried at Theberton, Suffolk.[23][24][25]
LZ96	L 49	June 13, 1917	Two reconnaissance missions around the North Sea; one raid on England dropping 2100 kg bombs; while returning, forced to land near Bourbonne-les-Bains on October 20, 1917 and captured almost undamaged by French forces. Plans derived from *LZ96* were later used in the United States for construction of the first US "zeppelin", the *USS Shenandoah (ZR-1)*.
LZ97	L 51	June 6, 1917	3 reconnaissance missions; one raid on the English coast, dropping 280 kg bombs. Destroyed in the Ahlhorn explosion (see *LZ87 "L 47"*).
LZ98	L 52	July 14, 1917	20 reconnaissance missions; accidentally placed above London by an unexpected storm during a raid, it dropped 2020 kg bombs there. Destroyed by its crew on June 23, 1919.
LZ99	L 54	August 13, 1917	14 reconnaissance missions; two attacks on England dropping 5840 kg bombs; destroyed together with *L 60* when seven British Sopwith Camel fighters from the first aircraft carrier, HMS *Furious*, bombed the halls in Tondern. (Only two fighters returned to the *Furious*, though three of the others landed in Denmark after running low on fuel.)
LZ100	L 53	August 8, 1917	19 reconnaissance missions; 4 attacks on England, dropping 11,930 kg bombs. Intercepted and destroyed by British Sopwith Camel N6812 flown by Lt Culley RAF, who took off from a lighter towed by the destroyer HMS *Redoubt*, on August 11, 1918
LZ101	L 55	September 1, 1917	Two attacks dropping 5450 kg bombs. Heavily damaged in the second one on October 19, 1917, it drifted behind western front and rose to Zeppelin all-time world record altitude of 7600 m to escape; then dismantled upon forced landing.

List of Zeppelins

LZ102	L 57	September 26, 1917	Not used in combat; foreseen for engagement in Africa. Damaged beyond repair by heavy wind on October 8, 1917.
LZ103	L 56	September 24, 1917	17 reconnaissance missions; participated in the last raid on England on August 6, 1918. Destroyed by its crew on June 23, 1919.
LZ104	L 59	October 30, 1917	LZ 104 Known as *das Afrika-Schiff*, stationed in Yambol (Bulgaria); L 59 started out on a mission to resupply German troops in German East Africa, but turned back upon (false) reports of a German surrender; nevertheless, the ship broke a long-distance flight record (6757 km in 95 hours and 5 minutes). One attack on Naples, Italy dropped 6400 kg of bombs. Crashed during a raid on Malta on April 7, 1918 for unknown reasons.
LZ105	L 58	October 29, 1917	Two reconnaissance missions; destroyed in the Ahlhorn explosion (see *LZ87 "L 47"*)
LZ106	L 61	December 12, 1917	9 reconnaissance missions; two attacks on England dropping 4500 kg bombs; in 1920 ordered to be transferred to Italy in the context of war reparations.
LZ107	L 62	January 19, 1918	Two reconnaissance missions; two attacks on England dropping 5923 kg bombs; on the raid on 12/13 April 1918 her gunners managed to damage and drive away an attacking airplane, the only known instance of this happening. Crashed north of Helgoland on May 10, 1918: shot down by Felixstowe F2A flying-boat N4291, Capt TC Pattinson and Capt TH Munday.[26]
LZ108	L 60	December 18, 1917	11 reconnaissance missions; one attack on England dropping 3,120 kg of bombs; destroyed together with *L 54* when British Sopwith Camel fighters launched from the aircraft carrier HMS Furious bombed the halls.
LZ109	L 64	March 11, 1918	13 reconnaissance missions over the North Sea; with L60, L61, L62, and L63 raided north England dropping 2800 kg in bombs. In 1920 transferred to England as war reparations. Scrapped at short notice when hangar required for the damaged British R36.[27]
LZ110	L 63	March 4, 1918	Dropped 8915 kg bombs in three attacks on England, including participation in the last raid on England on August 6, 1918. Destroyed by its crew on June 23, 1919.
LZ111	L 65	April 17, 1918	Participated in last raid on England on August 6, 1918. Destroyed by its crew on June 23, 1919.
LZ112	L 70	July 1, 1918	Directed last raid on England on August 6, 1918, with KK Peter Strasser, Commander of the Navy Airship Department on board; intercepted and destroyed over North Sea by British DeHavilland DH-4 flown by Major Egbert Cadbury with Captain Robert Leckie (later Air Vice-Marshal) as gunner.[28] Both these men shot down two Zeppelins: prior to L70, Cadbury had downed L21 and Leckie, L22.
LZ113	L 71	July 29, 1918	Not used in war; in 1920 ordered to be transferred to England in the context of war reparations. Scrapped at short notice when hangar required for the damaged British R36.
LZ114	L 72; in France: "Dixmude"	February 9, 1920	Not delivered because war ended; in 1920 ordered to be transferred to France in the context of war reparations and handed over on 9 July 1920 and renamed *Dixmude*.[29] Made then world record duration flight of 118 hours.[6] Vanished over Mediterranean in December 1923 killing all aboard.[29]
LZ115			*Not constructed*
LZ116			*Not constructed*
LZ117			*Not constructed*

List of Zeppelins

LZ118	Not constructed
LZ119	Not constructed

Zeppelins constructed after World War I

Production number	Name	Usage	First flight	Remarks	Image
LZ120	"Bodensee"; in Italy: "Esperia"	civilian; in Italy: ?	August 20, 1919	Included a first-class passenger section; used by DELAG until 1921, then ordered to be transferred to Italy in the context of war reparations.	
LZ121	"Nordstern"; in France: "Méditerranée"	civilian (intended); in France: ?	June 13, 1921	Intended for regular flights to Stockholm; ordered to be transferred to France in the context of war reparations.	
LZ122				not realized	
LZ123				not realized	
LZ124				not realized (construction forbidden by World War I Allied Powers)	
LZ125				not realized	
LZ126	ZR-3, USS *Los Angeles* (in the United States)	experimental, military	August 27, 1924	Ordered by the United States; transferred from Friedrichshafen to Lakehurst in 81 hours and 2 minutes, arriving on October 15, 1924, 9:52. Most successful US airship. Dismantled in August 1940.	
LZ127	"→ Graf Zeppelin"	civilian	September 18, 1928	Most successful airship in history; regular flights to North and South America; world tour in 1929, Arctic trip in 1931. Dismantled in 1940 upon order of Hermann Göring.	
LZ128				Project abandoned in favor of LZ129	
LZ129	"Hindenburg"	civilian	March 4, 1936	Intended for filling with helium gas instead of flammable hydrogen, which was, however, refused to be provided to Germany mainly by the US. Regular voyages to North and South America. Destroyed in Hindenburg disaster on May 6, 1937.	
LZ130	"→ Graf Zeppelin II"	civilian	September 14, 1938	Total 30 flights (36,550 km, 409 hrs), mainly flight testing but also electronic warfare and radio interception over English coast and Polish/German border. Modified for helium, but none provided by US. Last flight August 20, 1939. Dismantled in 1940 upon order of Hermann Göring.	
LZ131				not finished	

References

- The Airship Heritage Trust. L64 - LZ 109 "V" Class Super Zeppelin [30]
- Bruce, J.M. *Sopwith Pup: Historic Military Aircraft No 6* [31]. *Flight*. 1 January 1954. p. 8-12.
- Dooley, Sean C., *The Development of Material-Adapted Structural Form* [69] *- Part II: Appendices* [70]. THÈSE NO 2986 (2004), École Polytechnique Fédérale de Lausanne
- Eckener, Hugo. 1938. *Count Zeppelin: The Man and His Work*, translated by Leigh Fanell, London -- Massie Publishing Company, Ltd. -- (ASIN: B00085KPWK) (online extract pages 155-157, 210-211 [27])
- Lehmann, Ernst A.; Mingos, Howard. 1927. *The Zeppelins. The Development of the Airship, with the Story of the Zepplins Air Raids in the World War*. Published by I. H. SEARS & COMPANY, Inc. New York International Clearinghouse for Hydrogen Based Commerce - Zepplins [32] (online chapters I to VII)
- Martin Lockwood, Young People - Somewhere over Essex [33], Essex Police Museum
- Lueger, Otto: *Lexikon der gesamten Technik und ihrer Hilfswissenschaften*, Bd. 1 Stuttgart, Leipzig 1920., S. 404-412. Luftschiff [34] (German) Retrieved 2008-07-27
- Post & Tele Museum - Luftskibet Kommer! [35] (requires Flash and Javascript)
- redkitebooks.co.uk. Aviation Archaeology [36], Zeppelin L48 excavation carried out for BBC television
- redkitebooks.co.uk. The excavation of L48 the "Theberton Zeppelin" [37]. post-excavation report
- Rimmell, Ray; Preston, Tony. PAST ZEPPELIN L48 PHOTO OF THE MONTH. Theberton and Eastbridge Parish Council. 2008-07-27. URL:http://www.onesuffolk.co.uk/NR/rdonlyres/ 4EA8A481-F0DE-429A-B9AB-C0A0480FC99A/152695/Z1.doc.Accessed: 2008-07-27. (Archived by WebCite at http://www.webcitation.org/5ZdBiUBed) (Word document) from The Last Flight of the L48, linked from Theberton and Eastbridge Parish Council History [38].
- Thetford, Owen. *British Naval Aircraft since 1912*. London: Putnam, Fourth edition, 1978. ISBN 0-370-30021-1.
- www.theberton.info/timewatch.htm, Zeppelin, German zeppelin pictures, L48, LZ95, zeppelin crash ... [39]

Further reading

- Airships.net [45] Detailed nformation and photographs (interior and exterior), primarily about commercial Zeppelins
- eZEP.de [40] — The webportal for Zeppelin mail and airship memorabilia
- Zeppelin Study Group [41] — Research group for airship memorabilia and Zeppelin mail
- silhoeuttes of important Zeppelins from 1900 to 1919 [42], Lueger 1904–1920, shows LZ: 1,3,5,6,8,10,13,14,18,21,23,25,26,36,40,59,62,91,94,95,100,104,113,120
- Important airship types [43], Lueger 1904–1920, Table 1 lists data on selected Zeppelins

References

[1] Dooley A.197-A.200
[2] Janes's Pocket Book 7, Airship Development, p82
[3] Post & Tele Museum "Copenhagen - Count Zeppelin oversees everything from the gondola."
[4] http://www.uni-konstanz.de/FuF/Philo/Geschichte/MMAG/MMAG_Zeppelin/Elite/elite1.htm
[5] Lehmann Chapter I
[6] Lehmann Chapter II
[7] Lehmann Chapter V
[8] Thetford 1978, p.286.
[9] editors at de.wikipedia.org (http://de.wikipedia.org/wiki/Zeppelin#Der_erste_.E2.80.9EZeppelin.E2.80.9C)
[10] Lueger, Otto. 1920
[11] Lehmann Chapter IV
[12] " 1916 - 0744 (http://www.flightglobal.com/pdfarchive/view/1916/1916 - 0744.html)" (PDF). *Flight Magazine*: 740. 1916-08-31. . Retrieved 2009-09-25. "LZ 77 Révigny, France ... ... 21.2.1916".
[13] Thetford 1978, p.258.
[14] Lehmann Chapter V writes 12 tons total dropped in October 1915

[15] Rimmel. 1916 L11 crew photo - first photo shows Viktor Schütze was Korvettenkäpitan; of the L 48 crew only Otto Meith (died 1956-04-30) and Heinrich Ellerkamm (died 1963-08-04) eventually survived; Wilhelm Uecker died later from complications and influenza on 1918-11-11. Second photo shows British military salvage team posing in front of the wrecked L 48, note erroneous writing.

[16] " 1916 - 0185 (http://www.flightglobal.com/pdfarchive/view/1916/1916 - 0185.html)" (PDF). *Flight Magazine*: 185. 1916-03-02. . Retrieved 2009-09-25. "shooting down of the "L 77"".

[17] " 1916 - 0186 (http://www.flightglobal.com/pdfarchive/view/1916/1916 - 0186.html)" (PDF). *Flight Magazine*: 186. 1916-03-02. . Retrieved 2009-09-25. "8.30 p.m. that the airship was reported ... 6,000 ft. ... over Sommeille, using its searchlights for a brief moment. ... flew over Révigny ... The third shell, an incendiary one, found the target. ... came to earth slowly ... no explosion until the Zeppelin touched the ground ... seen by many ... from ... Révigny, ... village of Brabant-le-Roi ... Ten miles away, another Zeppelin, ... watched the fate of its companion and then turned and disappeared. At the same time a third Zeppelin flew over Lunéville and dropped bombs ... German source gives the following details ... carried over twenty of a crew, eight machine guns, and on the overhead platform two 'revolver' guns. Her orders were to bomb the railway junctions behind the front, especially, perhaps for its importance to Verdun (which is only some thirty miles away). ... three aeroplanes accompanied the Zeppelin.".

[18] http://www.uni-konstanz.de/FuF/Philo/Geschichte/MMAG/MMAG_Zeppelin/Alltag/alltag.htm

[19] *Inside Out investigates why air raid on Midlands led to British fisherman being accused of war crimes* (http://www.bbc.co.uk/pressoffice/pressreleases/stories/2005/02_february/15/io_airraids.shtml) BBC. 15 February 2005. Retrieved 30 July 2008

[20] Thetford 1978, p.80
[21] Bruce 1954, p.10.
[22] Martin Lockwood, Essex Police
[23] redkitebooks.co.uk
[24] redkitebooks.co.uk, post-excavation report
[25] www.theberton.info
[26] Thetford 1978, p.193-194.
[27] Airship Heritage Trust - L64
[28] Thetford 1978, p. 86.
[29] Bennighof, Mike (March 2006). " France's Naval Airship (http://www.avalanchepress.com/FrenchAirship.php)". . Retrieved 2009-09-25.
[30] http://www.aht.ndirect.co.uk/airships/l64/index.htm
[31] http://www.flightglobal.com/pdfarchive/view/1954/1954%20-%200016.html/The
[32] http://www.hydrogencommerce.com/zepplins/zepplins.htm#The%20Zeppelins
[33] http://www.essex.police.uk/offbeat/o_mu_20.php
[34] http://www.zeno.org/Lueger-1904/A/Luftschiff
[35] http://www.postogtelemuseet.dk/zeppex/en/routes/luftskib.html
[36] http://www.redkitebooks.co.uk/AA/ex06_L48_Theberton.html
[37] http://www.redkitebooks.co.uk/AA/ex06_L48_Post%20Excavation Report.html
[38] http://www.onesuffolk.co.uk/ThebertonPC/History/
[39] http://web.archive.org/web/20070704150613/www.theberton.info/timewatch.htm
[40] http://www.ezep.de/index.html
[41] http://www.ezep.de/zsg/zsg.html
[42] http://www.zeno.org/Lueger-1904.images/I/TL100565.jpg
[43] http://www.zeno.org/Lueger-1904.images/I/TL100564.jpg

Article Sources and Contributors

LZ 127 Graf Zeppelin *Source*: http://en.wikipedia.org/w/index.php?title=LZ_127_Graf_Zeppelin *Contributors*: 84user, Aille, Airship127, Akradecki, Aliter, Ardfern, Asclepias, Ashashyou, BartBenjamin, Blimpguy, Brianlanter, Bzuk, CRKingston, Centpacrr, Chrisjohnson, ChrisnHouston, Crum375, D6, Dgueiros, Eugene van der Pijll, F l a n k e r, F.bendik, Felicity4711, Globalphysics, Gobeirne, Grombo, Gsl, Guanaco, Hadhuey, Hugo999, Hux, Hydrargyrum, Imnotminkus, Ingolfson, J.Rohrer, John, John Reiher, Johntex, Jons63, Kammergericht, Ke4roh, Kjetil r, Lestatdelc, Lightmouse, Logawi, M.nelson, Manxruler, MarkHab, Martorell, Mav, MilborneOne, Mion, Moon light shadow, MrMarmite, Mrzaius, Mstuomel, NE2, Odaiba, PFHLai, Paradiso, Paul A, Pavel Vozenilek, Peter Delmonte, PeterTheWall, Petri Krohn, Phil in the 818, Pinot, Polemaco, RandomCritic, Randomekewaka, Rccoms, RedWolf, RichLindvall, Richard Weil, Rios, Rlandmann, Rodeime, Sam Hocevar, Sandius, Snowmanradio, Stan Shebs, Stepa, Stephan Schulz, Terrible Tim, TravellerDMT-07, Uriber, Wetman, Wikianon, 64 anonymous edits

Airship *Source*: http://en.wikipedia.org/w/index.php?title=Airship *Contributors*: .:Ajvol:., 16@r, 489thCorsica, 6birc, 84user, A2Kafir, A51Abductee, ABVR, AEROCRAT, Aarchiba, Abidder, Accurizer, Adimovk5, Admiral Valdemar, Aeros40D, Aerosml, Airshipman, Akradecki, AlainV, Alarics, Aleia.carameve, Aliter, Alkivar, Alligin, Altenmann, AmigaBob, Andrewa, Angenhariaus, Apoc2400, Apyule, Arbus Driver, Archaeopteryx, Aris Katsaris, Asmor, Astudent, Audiolessonover, AustinZ, Autodidactyl, Autopilot, Axeman89, Axlq, Aznime, BartBenjamin, Bear91602, Bellhalla, Benandorsqueaks, Benvenuto, Bill faulk, Binksternet, Blainster, BlankVerse, Blimpguy, Bobblewik, Bobbyboi, Bobfos, Bojac6, Bongwarrior, Booksworm, Brainfuck, BrianGeneral, Briangotts, Brucent, Bryan Derksen, Bublegun, Budwysor, Burgercat, CTSCo, Calair, Calm, Camembert, Cancun771, Catbar, Cbraga, Ccolting, CharlesC, Chris Buckey, Chris the speller, Cjewell, Cjrother, Cmdrjameson, Colin Rowat, Colonies Chris, CommonsDelinker, Communisthamster, Coop, Costyn, Cregq, Crum375, Cybersquid, Cédric, Danio, Davandron, Dave.Dunford, David Latapie, David R. Ingham, Dblecros, Deathphoenix, Deb, Dirac66, Dispenser, DocWatson42, Dpenguinman, Dyaa, Eassin, Ec5618, Ecozeppelin, Ecthelion83, Elipongo, Eliyahu S, Elodea87, Epbr123, Ericg, Errarel, Ezhiukas 7, F.bendik, Fairfieldfencer, Fede.Campana, Fenrir-of-the-Shadows, Flaviohmg, Foofbun, Fortdj33, Fredrik, Friedfish, GDM, GRAHAMUK, GVP Webmaster, Gadfium, Gaius Cornelius, Gapperjack, Gbleem, Gene Nygaard, Gene s, Gilliam, Glenn, Glenn Magus Harvey, Globalmindcollective, GraemeL, GraemeLeggett, Graham87, Graldensblud, Greyengine5, Grunt, Grutness, Gsl, Gtrmp, Guidomax, GunnarRene, Hadhuey, Haditahir, Henry W. Schmitt, HereToHelp, Herostratus, Highwind, Histrion, Hloyea, Hmains, Hooperbloob, Hotcrocodile, Hugo999, Ian Strachan, Icarus, Iceberg3k, Immblueversion, Intgr, Inwind, IronChris, Isaac Dupree, J-Star, JForget, JaGa, Jac16888, Jade Knight, JarlaxleArtemis, Javqui, Jcfregnan, Jim Jackson, Jkstark, JoJan, Joe N, Johnbibby, Jonathan.s.kt, Jondel, Joy, Jph2, JulieADriver, JuniperisCommunis, Jwissick, Jwolfe, Jyril, KVDP, Karl-Henner, KathrynLybarger, Kcordina, Keeshu, Keithp41, Kelly Martin, Kember, KnowledgeOfSelf, Knulclunk, Knutux, Kozuch, KrakatoaKatie, Ktr101, Kubanczyk, Kurykh, LA2, Lao Wai, Leandrod, Lee M, Leigh, Liftarn, Lightmouse, LilHelpa, Ling.Nut, Lockesdonkey, Logawi, Lzur, MER-C, Magiclite, Magus732, Mahjongg, Marek69, Mark Lincoln, MarkS, Martpol, Matthewedwards, Maury Markowitz, Mav, Mboverload, Mbutts, Mdhennessey, Me, Myself, and I, Meneth, Mervyn, Mhking, Michael Hardy, Michael Zimmermann, Micogobodo, Midgley, Mike Young, Mion, Mister Farkas, Mjmcb1, MoogleDan, Mormegil, Moshe Constantine Hassan Al-Silverburg, Mr Mulliner, Mrzaius, Mulad, Nabla, Nautical, NawlinWiki, Night Gyr, Niteowlneils, Nixer, Nono64, Not a dog, Noveltyghost, Olaf Davis, Olga Doktorova, Omegatron, Orangedayday, Oreckel, Oriolpont, Oroso, Oscarthecat, Ospalh, Ovo design, Oybubblejohn, Oydman, PHG, Pachakuti2012, Papaya07, Parsecboy, Patriarca12, Patrick, PatrickSalsbury, Patstuart, Pavel Vozenilek, Pdn, PeaceNT, Pedant17, Peng, Peterolo, Petmal, Pfahlstrom, Pgan002, Phoebe, Phoenix Hacker, Phoenix-wiki, Piano non troppo, Piledhigheranddeeper, Pilotguy, Pinot, Piotrus, Pkuxulu, PlaysInPeoria, Pmanderson, PoccilScript, Poli, Polynova, Quistnix, Qxz, Radak, RadicalBender, Radio Guy, Red Sunset, RedBLACKandBURN, RedWolf, Redvers, Reedy, Rees11, Rei, Researcher22, RexNL, Rich Farmbrough, Richard New Forest, Rigadoun, Rjwilmsi, Rl, Rlandmann, Rlest, Rls, Rmckay630, Rnb, RoyBoy, SDC, Saberwyn, Sam Hocevar, Sammy1339, Sandstein, Saperaud, Sardanaphalus, Scewing, SchfiftyThree, Scott Roy Atwood, Scriberius, Securiger, Selket, Semorrison, Sheridan, Sherurcij, Sigurdhu, Sirhanx2, Skald the Rhymer, Smithbrenon, Snowmanradio, Socrunningman, Soczyczi, Someguy1221, SpaceCaptain, SpaceFlight89, SpookyMulder, Steamfire, SteelersFan UK06, Stephan Leeds, Steve for life, Stormwatch, Suntzu3500, Swid, Taak, Tabletop, Tarquin, TarseeRota, Tassedethe, Template namespace initialisation script, Teoul, Th1rt3en, TheListUpdater, Theymos, Thingg, Thisgureat, Thrillseekr, Tide rolls, Timbouctou, Timeineurope, Timewatcher, TobyJ, Tomatensaft, Tony1, Tpbradbury, Transworldbmx, Treesock, Trevor MacInnis, Twilo, Unionhawk, Until It Sleeps, UtherSRG, VetPsychWars, Vilcxjo, Vreemdst, Wahkeenah, Wavehunter, Wetman, Whitepaw, Wikianon, Willem Tijssen, Willemtijssen, William13, Windharp, Winkler, Wolfkeeper, Wsk, Wyrdlight, Xanzzibar, Xhienne, Xyz-321, Yath, Ysoldak, Zuckyd1, Zxcvbnm, Zzyzx11, 504 anonymous edits

Ferdinand von Zeppelin *Source*: http://en.wikipedia.org/w/index.php?title=Ferdinand_von_Zeppelin *Contributors*: (, 84user, Alphachimp, Andre Engels, Ardfern, Attilios, AubreyEllenShomo, Az1568, Blimpguy, Borgx, Braaropolis, Brandon97, Britmax, Cburnett, Chris 73, Cube lurker, D6, DerHexer, Djmutex, Dylpickleh8, E-Kartoffel, Ed g2s, Elipongo, Epbr123, EugeneZelenko, Folksong, Frankyboy5, Fuzheado, Gaelen S., Gaff, Gerhard51, Gestumblindi, Giro720, Gkklein, Golf Bravo, GraemeLeggett, Gryffindor, Gunter, Guy Peters, Guyster, Hacktivist, Hadhuey, Hephaestos, Hqb, Immortal Wowbagger, IndulgentReader, Infrogmation, Isnow, J.delanoy, Jeffkw, John, Johntex, Jpbowen, Jrcla2, Julius.kusuma, Kicka, Kirby-oh, Kubiwan, Kurt Leyman, LAX, MSJapan, Magi Media, Masterchi101, Mendaliv, Mion, Mister Farkas, Mitico, Mrdice, Mu, N1RK4UDSK714, Nborders1972, Nebulousecho, Nicapicella, Ninja KnightxX, Oerjan, Olessi, Paranomia, Paul A, Pavel Vozenilek, Perl, Princeaeneas, Pseudomonas, Qaqaq, Rbeard, RexNL, Richard Arthur Norton (1958-), RobNS, RobertG, Routerrandy4, Sam Hocevar, Scoop100, Sdrawkcab, ShelfSkewed, Shell Kinney, Sicilianmandolin, Snigbrook, Soulhunter74, Spankmymonkeyharder, Spencer, Stern, Suruena, Teodorico, Thingg, Thrindel, Tohru Honda13, Wik, Woohookitty, XXL2oo, Zedlik, Zoe, Zro, ßurns, 119 anonymous edits

Graf *Source*: http://en.wikipedia.org/w/index.php?title=Graf *Contributors*: Adam Bishop, Ahoerstemeier, Altenmann, Andre Engels, AndrewHowse, Apoivre, Arcarius, Arch dude, Barticus88, Betalicious, CdaMVvWgS, Charles, Charles Matthews, Chl, Cladeal832, Correct & improve, Countakeshi, D6, Dbachmann, Dieter Simon, DocWatson42, Docu, Dominus, DrKiernan, Earle Martin, Edward321, FactStraight, Fastifex, Funkymonks, Gerhard51, GreatWhiteNortherner, Harpercollege, HoboChunk, JJL, JWhitaker106, Janejellyroll, John Kenney, Joy, Jpbrenna, KF, Kmorozov, Kris ether, Larsw, Laurens-af, Ligulem, LittleOldMe, Lord Emsworth, Mackensen, Marcika, Martg76, MeekSaffron, Mic, Minesweeper, Nightmist, Nikai, Old Moonraker, Olessi, Origoventus, OwenBlacker, PWilkinson, Pagetools, Pearle, Pedant17, Pelagus, Perey, RafaAzevedo, RedWolf, Rjwilmsi, Rrostrom, Ruhrjung, Saga City, Santryl, Shell Kinney, Shot info, Spasemunki, StanZegel, Stijn Calle, Supparluca, Thomas Ludwig, Trigaranus, Wetman, Writtenright, Zocky, 47 anonymous edits

Hugo Eckener *Source*: http://en.wikipedia.org/w/index.php?title=Hugo_Eckener *Contributors*: 84user, A. B., Airship127, Aldis90, Alethe, Blimpguy, Catsmeat, D6, Dimadick, Dj manton, DrGeoduck, Drbreznjev, Frankyboy5, Gerhard51, Glatisant, Hadhuey, Hooperbloob, Hugo-cs, Il palazzo, Jengod, John, John Paul Parks, Jsan, Jwalte04, KF, KPH2293, Kevin Breitenstein, Kevinkor2, Kinneyboy90, LilHelpa, Logawi, Mark T, Michael Patrick Wilson, Mikeblas, Mister Farkas, Mu, Njruk, Olessi, Paul A, Pizzazzle, Richard Weil, Rjwilmsi, Rlandmann, Snoyes, Staffelde, Trotboy, Wik, Wikianon, 51 anonymous edits

Maybach *Source*: http://en.wikipedia.org/w/index.php?title=Maybach *Contributors*: A Friendly Nerd, AAA!, ABF, Acela Express, Adamthegenius, Andy odell, Animum, Ardfern, Arthena, Astamanana, BSI, Bardhylius, Barkinkurt, Bdesham, Bell'Orso, Benwildeboer, Biker Biker, Bjelleklang, Bloodless, Bogdangiusca, Bomac, BrendelSignature, Brossow, Bucinka, Bud001, Bumcheekcity, CZmarlin, Can't sleep, clown will eat me, CanadianLinuxUser, Cbarnes3, Chaparral2J, Chowbok, Cjjanmb, Clawson, CommonsDelinker, Creator7, CrnaGora, Csaba Jancsovics, D3v4st4t0r, DagnyB, DanMS, David Latapie, DavidFarmbrough, Dawidl, Delivi, DerHexer, Diosnoche, DocWatson42, Dogcow, Dostwo, DrDentz, Dysprosia, E.P.I.C., Edal, Elsonlau, Enotayokel, FerdinandFrog, FunPika, Gadget17, Garzo, GraemeLeggett, Gryffindor, Guccipuppy100, Gurklurk, Gwross, Harald Hansen, Hasannur, Hektor, Hmette, Hu12, Hugo999, JFreeman, JFseekingtruth, JKfromtheSK, JanDaMan, Jaraalbe, Jarbru, Jeff3000, Jgp, JiVE, Just Another Dan, Kmorozov, Kwamikagami, Leonard G., Lester, Lightmouse, Luxemont, Mac, Magnus.de, Mahidol, Manop, Marcika, MarkusHagenlocher, Matt Gies, Meelar, Meemonkeyman, Millisits, Mimihitam, Mohanjith, Mstuomel, Mulad, Myscrnnm, Nard the Bard, Niffux, Nimbus227, Nrbelex, Old Guard, Parkjunwung, Petadeo, PubliusFL, Quadzilla99, RJASE1, RadicalBender, RobDe68, SDC, SElefant, SWAdair, Salam32, Senators, Sfoskett, Shawn, Sidewayslion, Slgrandson, Sporath, Stephan Leeds, Stewacide, Superman7658, THEunique, TOBY49, Tempodivalse, Teutonic Tamer, Texture, That Guy, From That Show!, Thomas Veil, Thraxas, Tomh009, Travis Hiscock, Turk oğlan, Typ932, Typhoonchaser, Vlad, Walshga, Weiteck, Wikipediarules2221, Wimt, Wittkowsky, Wurblzap, Xiahou, Yidisheryid, Youmils03, Zach4636, Zyance, Zzzzzzus, СЛУЖБА, 220 anonymous edits

Buoyancy compensator (aviation) *Source*: http://en.wikipedia.org/w/index.php?title=Buoyancy_compensator_%28aviation%29 *Contributors*: 84user, Bob Burkhardt, Mion, The PIPE, 2 anonymous edits

LZ 130 Graf Zeppelin *Source*: http://en.wikipedia.org/w/index.php?title=LZ_130_Graf_Zeppelin *Contributors*: 84user, A2Kafir, Akradecki, Ardfern, Centpacrr, Chris the speller, Frankyboy5, Hadhuey, Hugo999, JHFTC, Jim Jackson, JoanneB, John, Karlwk, Kriscotta, Logawi, Michael Hobi, Michael Zimmermann, MilborneOne, Mion, Nimbus227, Odaiba, Paul A, Petri Krohn, Rlandmann, Wikianon, Zenibo, 20 anonymous edits

List of Zeppelins *Source*: http://en.wikipedia.org/w/index.php?title=List_of_Zeppelins *Contributors*: -js-, 84user, A2Kafir, Adrian Roberts, Adrian roberts, Ardfern, Benvenuto, Bihco, Bill faulk, Blimpguy, Bobblewik, Bogdangiusca, Boothferry, Brequinda, Cargocontainer, Catsmeat, Choess, Chowbok, Colonies Chris, Docu, Erudy, Frymaster, Gene Nygaard, GraemeLeggett, Gsl, Hacktivist, Hadhuey, Intangir, IsarSteve, J.Rohrer, Jeffmatt, John, Karl Dickman, Ken Gallager, Ketiltrout, Krellis, Larzac1, Logawi, Maralia, Mark Sublette, Markussep, Meddlin' Pedant, Megaversal, Mervyn, Mr Stephen, Nashikawa, Neckro, Nigel Ish, Nono64, Odaiba, Ouro, PBP, Paul A, Pavel Vozenilek, Rccoms, Red Sunset, Reuben, Rich257, Rjwilmsi, RobertWalden, Rossami, Saga City, Sannse, Scoop100, Shanel, Smarkflea, Spearhead, Tabletop, The Saturday Boy, Trevor MacInnis, Triwbe, Wikianon, Winkler, Zanoni, 42 anonymous edits

Image Sources, Licenses and Contributors

Image:ZeppelinLZ127a.jpg *Source*: http://en.wikipedia.org/w/index.php?title=File:ZeppelinLZ127a.jpg *License*: unknown *Contributors*: user:Grombo

File:Bundesarchiv Bild 102-00834, Friedrichshafen, Luftschiff Graf Zeppelin 127 highlighted construction.png *Source*: http://en.wikipedia.org/w/index.php?title=File:Bundesarchiv_Bild_102-00834,_Friedrichshafen,_Luftschiff_Graf_Zeppelin_127_highlighted_construction.png *License*: unknown *Contributors*: User:84user

Image:Cercle rouge 50%.svg *Source*: http://en.wikipedia.org/w/index.php?title=File:Cercle_rouge_50%.svg *License*: Public Domain *Contributors*: Finnrind, PoM, Rimshot, Rocket000, STyx, Wikid77

Image:ZeppelinLZ127b.jpg *Source*: http://en.wikipedia.org/w/index.php?title=File:ZeppelinLZ127b.jpg *License*: unknown *Contributors*: user:Grombo

Image:Torre do Zeppelin - Jiquia - Recife.JPG *Source*: http://en.wikipedia.org/w/index.php?title=File:Torre_do_Zeppelin_-_Jiquia_-_Recife.JPG *License*: Public Domain *Contributors*: User:Lsouza7

Image:Graf Zeppelin 1930 Helsinki.jpg *Source*: http://en.wikipedia.org/w/index.php?title=File:Graf_Zeppelin_1930_Helsinki.jpg *License*: Public Domain *Contributors*: Sulo Tuomela

Image:Graf Zeppelin First North American Flight 1928.jpg *Source*: http://en.wikipedia.org/w/index.php?title=File:Graf_Zeppelin_First_North_American_Flight_1928.jpg *License*: unknown *Contributors*: 84user, Centpacrr, MilborneOne

Image:DLZ 127 Graf Zeppelin Fabric.jpg *Source*: http://en.wikipedia.org/w/index.php?title=File:DLZ_127_Graf_Zeppelin_Fabric.jpg *License*: unknown *Contributors*: Original uploader was Centpacrr at en.wikipedia

Image:Interrupted Flight 1929.jpg *Source*: http://en.wikipedia.org/w/index.php?title=File:Interrupted_Flight_1929.jpg *License*: unknown *Contributors*: 84user, Centpacrr, MilborneOne

Image:Weltrundfahrt Map 1929.jpg *Source*: http://en.wikipedia.org/w/index.php?title=File:Weltrundfahrt_Map_1929.jpg *License*: GNU Lesser General Public License *Contributors*: User:Rlandmann

Image:DLZ127 Round the World 1929.jpg *Source*: http://en.wikipedia.org/w/index.php?title=File:DLZ_127_Round_the_World_1929.jpg *License*: Public Domain *Contributors*: Original uploader was Centpacrr at en.wikipedia

Image:Graf Zeppelin 3 Reichsmark 1930.jpg *Source*: http://en.wikipedia.org/w/index.php?title=File:Graf_Zeppelin_3_Reichsmark_1930.jpg *License*: Public Domain *Contributors*: 84user, Centpacrr, MilborneOne

Image:Graf Zeppelin Polar Flight 1931.jpg *Source*: http://en.wikipedia.org/w/index.php?title=File:Graf_Zeppelin_Polar_Flight_1931.jpg *License*: Public Domain *Contributors*: 84user, Centpacrr, MilborneOne

Image:Zeppelinmarke Polarf.jpg *Source*: http://en.wikipedia.org/w/index.php?title=File:Zeppelinmarke_Polarf.jpg *License*: unknown *Contributors*: BLueFiSH.as, Butko, ChristianBier, Felix Stember, GrahamBould, Kneiphof, Maksim, Stan Shebs, Xenophon

Image:Mittelmeerfahrt 1929.jpg *Source*: http://en.wikipedia.org/w/index.php?title=File:Mittelmeerfahrt_1929.jpg *License*: unknown *Contributors*: 84user, Centpacrr

Image:The Graf Zeppelin's rendezvous with pyramids of Gizeh, Egypt.jpg *Source*: http://en.wikipedia.org/w/index.php?title=File:The_Graf_Zeppelin's_rendezvous_with_pyramids_of_Gizeh,_Egypt.jpg *License*: Public Domain *Contributors*: Keystone View Company

Image:Zeppelin Passenger Pins.jpg *Source*: http://en.wikipedia.org/w/index.php?title=File:Zeppelin_Passenger_Pins.jpg *License*: unknown *Contributors*: 84user, Centpacrr, MilborneOne

Image:1934 "Graf Zeppelin" South America Schedule.jpg *Source*: http://en.wikipedia.org/w/index.php?title=File:1934_"Graf_Zeppelin"_South_America_Schedule.jpg *License*: unknown *Contributors*: 84user, Centpacrr, MilborneOne, Thingg, Undead warrior

Image:D-LZ127 First South America Flight 1934.jpg *Source*: http://en.wikipedia.org/w/index.php?title=File:D-LZ127_First_South_America_Flight_1934.jpg *License*: unknown *Contributors*: Original uploader was Centpacrr at en.wikipedia

Image:Stamp US 1930 65c.jpg *Source*: http://en.wikipedia.org/w/index.php?title=File:Stamp_US_1930_65c.jpg *License*: Public Domain *Contributors*: United States Postal Service

File:Zeppelin-LZ-127 internal and gas cells.svg *Source*: http://en.wikipedia.org/w/index.php?title=File:Zeppelin-LZ-127_internal_and_gas_cells.svg *License*: Public Domain *Contributors*: User:84user, User:Thyes

File:Brockhaus-Efron Aeronavtika.jpg *Source*: http://en.wikipedia.org/w/index.php?title=File:Brockhaus-Efron_Aeronavtika.jpg *License*: Public Domain *Contributors*: unknown

Image:USS Akron in flight, nov 1931.jpg *Source*: http://en.wikipedia.org/w/index.php?title=File:USS_Akron_in_flight,_nov_1931.jpg *License*: Public Domain *Contributors*: 84user, Dcoetzee, Editor at Large, Idot, PMG, Quistnix, Saperaud

Image:Usn-airships.jpg *Source*: http://en.wikipedia.org/w/index.php?title=File:Usn-airships.jpg *License*: Public Domain *Contributors*: 84user, Carnildo, Saperaud, 1 anonymous edits

Image:BlanchardChannelFlight.jpg *Source*: http://en.wikipedia.org/w/index.php?title=File:BlanchardChannelFlight.jpg *License*: unknown *Contributors*: Olivier2, PHGCOM

Image:GiffardAirship.JPG *Source*: http://en.wikipedia.org/w/index.php?title=File:GiffardAirship.JPG *License*: Public Domain *Contributors*: User:Mike Young

Image:DupuyLomeDirigeable.jpg *Source*: http://en.wikipedia.org/w/index.php?title=File:DupuyLomeDirigeable.jpg *License*: Public Domain *Contributors*: Kneiphof, Mu, PHGCOM

Image:Sd num6 rounding tower.jpg *Source*: http://en.wikipedia.org/w/index.php?title=File:Sd_num6_rounding_tower.jpg *License*: Public Domain *Contributors*: Original uploader was Blimpguy at en.wikipedia

File:Type R Observation Balloon.jpg *Source*: http://en.wikipedia.org/w/index.php?title=File:Type_R_Observation_Balloon.jpg *License*: Public Domain *Contributors*: Los Angeles Times

Image:1918 view from French dirigible.jpg *Source*: http://en.wikipedia.org/w/index.php?title=File:1918_view_from_French_dirigible.jpg *License*: Public Domain *Contributors*: Not given

Image:R-38-rescue.jpg *Source*: http://en.wikipedia.org/w/index.php?title=File:R-38-rescue.jpg *License*: GNU Free Documentation License *Contributors*: US Navy

Image:USS Shenandoah Bau.jpg *Source*: http://en.wikipedia.org/w/index.php?title=File:USS_Shenandoah_Bau.jpg *License*: Public Domain *Contributors*: Edward, Saperaud

Image:Zeppelin.jpg *Source*: http://en.wikipedia.org/w/index.php?title=File:Zeppelin.jpg *License*: Public Domain *Contributors*: NASA Ames Research Center (NASA-ARC)

Image:Uss-akron-manhattan.jpg *Source*: http://en.wikipedia.org/w/index.php?title=File:Uss-akron-manhattan.jpg *License*: Public Domain *Contributors*: Unknown?

Image:Hindenburg burning.jpg *Source*: http://en.wikipedia.org/w/index.php?title=File:Hindenburg_burning.jpg *License*: Public Domain *Contributors*: Murray Becker

File:Goodyear ZNPK (K-28) Puritan (2834542477).jpg *Source*: http://en.wikipedia.org/w/index.php?title=File:Goodyear_ZNPK_(K-28)_Puritan_(2834542477).jpg *License*: Creative Commons Attribution 2.0 *Contributors*: Cliff from I now live in Arlington, VA (Outside Washington DC), USA

Image:mcastustin1.jpg *Source*: http://en.wikipedia.org/w/index.php?title=File:Mcastustin1.jpg *License*: Public Domain *Contributors*: Original uploader was Lordkinbote at en.wikipedia

Image:USN ZP-14 Blimp at RAF Gibraltar 1944.jpg *Source*: http://en.wikipedia.org/w/index.php?title=File:USN_ZP-14_Blimp_at_RAF_Gibraltar_1944.jpg *License*: Public Domain *Contributors*: 489thCorsica

Image:Goodyear blimp.jpg *Source*: http://en.wikipedia.org/w/index.php?title=File:Goodyear_blimp.jpg *License*: GNU Free Documentation License *Contributors*: User:Wars

Image:Spiritofdubai.jpg *Source*: http://en.wikipedia.org/w/index.php?title=File:Spiritofdubai.jpg *License*: Creative Commons Attribution-Sharealike 2.5 *Contributors*: Sfan00 IMG, WyrdIight

Image:Prallluftschiff 01 KMJ.jpg *Source*: http://en.wikipedia.org/w/index.php?title=File:Prallluftschiff_01_KMJ.jpg *License*: GNU Free Documentation License *Contributors*: MB-one, Morio, Saperaud

Image:Zeppelin NT im Flug.jpg *Source*: http://en.wikipedia.org/w/index.php?title=File:Zeppelin_NT_im_Flug.jpg *License*: GNU Free Documentation License *Contributors*: Blurpeace, Crux, Hadhuey, Ikiwaner, Schekinov Alexey Victorovich

Image:Ferdinand von Zeppelin.jpg *Source*: http://en.wikipedia.org/w/index.php?title=File:Ferdinand_von_Zeppelin.jpg *License*: Public Domain *Contributors*: Butko, John Vandenberg, Petrusbarbygere, Topory

File:Bundesarchiv Bild 146-1986-128-10, Isabella Gräfin von Zeppelin.jpg *Source*: http://en.wikipedia.org/w/index.php?title=File:Bundesarchiv_Bild_146-1986-128-10,_Isabella_Gräfin_von_Zeppelin.jpg *License*: unknown *Contributors*: Vogelsang, E. (Frau)

File:Hauptmann Graf Zeppelin.jpg *Source*: http://en.wikipedia.org/w/index.php?title=File:Hauptmann_Graf_Zeppelin.jpg *License*: Public Domain *Contributors*: Richard Brend'amour, 1831 - 1915

File:Bundesarchiv Bild 146-1972-099-15, Ferdinand Graf Zeppelin am Schreibtisch.jpg *Source*: http://en.wikipedia.org/w/index.php?title=File:Bundesarchiv_Bild_146-1972-099-15,_Ferdinand_Graf_Zeppelin_am_Schreibtisch.jpg *License*: unknown *Contributors*: Felix Stember

File:Graf zeppelin bueste 01.jpg *Source*: http://en.wikipedia.org/w/index.php?title=File:Graf_zeppelin_bueste_01.jpg *License*: Creative Commons Attribution-Sharealike 2.5 *Contributors*: User:Raboe001

Image:Hugo Eckener.jpg *Source*: http://en.wikipedia.org/w/index.php?title=File:Hugo_Eckener.jpg *License*: Public Domain *Contributors*: Unknown (National Photo Company)

Image Sources, Licenses and Contributors

File:Bundesarchiv Bild 102-00645, Probefahrt des Zeppelin-Luftschiffes Z.R. III.jpg *Source*: http://en.wikipedia.org/w/index.php?title=File:Bundesarchiv_Bild_102-00645,_Probefahrt_des_Zeppelin-Luftschiffes_Z.R._III.jpg *License*: unknown *Contributors*: 84user, Regenschirmwetter

File:Bundesarchiv Bild 102-12053, Rudolf Lasarewitsch Samoilowitsch und Hugo Eckener.jpg *Source*: http://en.wikipedia.org/w/index.php?title=File:Bundesarchiv_Bild_102-12053,_Rudolf_Lasarewitsch_Samoilowitsch_und_Hugo_Eckener.jpg *License*: unknown *Contributors*: 84user, Origamiemensch

Image:BremenHoetgerHdG09.jpg *Source*: http://en.wikipedia.org/w/index.php?title=File:BremenHoetgerHdG09.jpg *License*: Creative Commons Attribution-Sharealike 2.0 *Contributors*: Jürgen Howaldt

Image:commons-logo.svg *Source*: http://en.wikipedia.org/w/index.php?title=File:Commons-logo.svg *License*: logo *Contributors*: Harryboyles, RockMFR, Stephen Bain

Image:Maybach.png *Source*: http://en.wikipedia.org/w/index.php?title=File:Maybach.png *License*: unknown *Contributors*: Avala, Bkell, Hektor, Malcolma, RadicalBender, SeventyThree, Stan Shebs

Image:Maybach-Limousine.jpg *Source*: http://en.wikipedia.org/w/index.php?title=File:Maybach-Limousine.jpg *License*: GNU Free Documentation License *Contributors*: Wilfried Wittkowsky - User Wittkowsky on de.wikipedia

Image:Maybach Storm Gun.jpg *Source*: http://en.wikipedia.org/w/index.php?title=File:Maybach_Storm_Gun.jpg *License*: unknown *Contributors*: User:Edal

Image:Reklama Maybach W3.jpg *Source*: http://en.wikipedia.org/w/index.php?title=File:Reklama_Maybach_W3.jpg *License*: GNU Free Documentation License *Contributors*: Jackcorporation

Image:Maybach 62 BMK.jpg *Source*: http://en.wikipedia.org/w/index.php?title=File:Maybach_62_BMK.jpg *License*: unknown *Contributors*: User:BMK

Image:Maybachs.JPG *Source*: http://en.wikipedia.org/w/index.php?title=File:Maybachs.JPG *License*: unknown *Contributors*: User:Brendel

Image:Excelero.jpg *Source*: http://en.wikipedia.org/w/index.php?title=File:Excelero.jpg *License*: Creative Commons Attribution 2.0 *Contributors*: Simon Davison from Los Gatos, United States

Image:USS Macon F9C.jpg *Source*: http://en.wikipedia.org/w/index.php?title=File:USS_Macon_F9C.jpg *License*: Public Domain *Contributors*: USN

Image:LZ130-Bugspitze WL.jpg *Source*: http://en.wikipedia.org/w/index.php?title=File:LZ130-Bugspitze_WL.jpg *License*: Creative Commons Attribution 2.5 *Contributors*: Original uploader was Willy Logan at en.wikipedia

Image:Graf Zeppelin II 1938.jpg *Source*: http://en.wikipedia.org/w/index.php?title=File:Graf_Zeppelin_II_1938.jpg *License*: unknown *Contributors*: DigitalImageServices.com (Digital image)

Image:First Zeppelin ascent.jpg *Source*: http://en.wikipedia.org/w/index.php?title=File:First_Zeppelin_ascent.jpg *License*: Public Domain *Contributors*: Chris 73, Daniel 1992, Haukurth, Mutter Erde, Quistnix, Saperaud

File:Bundesarchiv Bild 183-R27054, Graf Zeppelin mit Tochter im Luftschiff LZ 3.jpg *Source*: http://en.wikipedia.org/w/index.php?title=File:Bundesarchiv_Bild_183-R27054,_Graf_Zeppelin_mit_Tochter_im_Luftschiff_LZ_3.jpg *License*: unknown *Contributors*: 84user, Felix Stember

Image:Zeppelin LZ4.jpg *Source*: http://en.wikipedia.org/w/index.php?title=File:Zeppelin_LZ4.jpg *License*: Public Domain *Contributors*: Chris 73, Quistnix, Saperaud, Siebrand

File:Bundesarchiv Bild 146-1978-101-14, Zeppelin Katastrophe in Weilburg.jpg *Source*: http://en.wikipedia.org/w/index.php?title=File:Bundesarchiv_Bild_146-1978-101-14,_Zeppelin_Katastrophe_in_Weilburg.jpg *License*: unknown *Contributors*: Felix Stember

File:Bundesarchiv Bild 146-1970-077-20, Berlin, Landung des Zeppelin LZ 6.jpg *Source*: http://en.wikipedia.org/w/index.php?title=File:Bundesarchiv_Bild_146-1970-077-20,_Berlin,_Landung_des_Zeppelin_LZ_6.jpg *License*: unknown *Contributors*: Felix Stember, 1 anonymous edits

Image:LZ7 passenger zeppelin mod.jpg *Source*: http://en.wikipedia.org/w/index.php?title=File:LZ7_passenger_zeppelin_mod.jpg *License*: Public Domain *Contributors*: User:Andro96

Image:1911.06.26 Schwaben.jpl.jpg *Source*: http://en.wikipedia.org/w/index.php?title=File:1911.06.26_Schwaben_jpl.jpg *License*: Public Domain *Contributors*: Jed, Quistnix, Saperaud

Image:LZ11 Viktoria Luise.jpg *Source*: http://en.wikipedia.org/w/index.php?title=File:LZ11_Viktoria_Luise.jpg *License*: Public Domain *Contributors*: Quistnix, Rcbutcher, Saperaud, Siebrand

Image:Zeppelin III in flight.jpg *Source*: http://en.wikipedia.org/w/index.php?title=File:Zeppelin_III_in_flight.jpg *License*: Public Domain *Contributors*: Bain News Service, publisher.

Image:1912 Hansa jpl.jpg *Source*: http://en.wikipedia.org/w/index.php?title=File:1912_Hansa_jpl.jpg *License*: Public Domain *Contributors*: Jed, Quistnix, Saperaud

Image:1913.04.03 ZIV Luneville 1 jpl.jpg *Source*: http://en.wikipedia.org/w/index.php?title=File:1913.04.03_ZIV_Luneville_1_jpl.jpg *License*: Public Domain *Contributors*: Baronnet, Jed, Quistnix, Saperaud

Image:Crash Zeppelin LZ18 (LII).jpg *Source*: http://en.wikipedia.org/w/index.php?title=File:Crash_Zeppelin_LZ18_(LII).jpg *License*: Public Domain *Contributors*: 84user, Man vyi, Quistnix, Saperaud

Image:1916.05.03 L20 3 jpl.jpg *Source*: http://en.wikipedia.org/w/index.php?title=File:1916.05.03_L20_3_jpl.jpg *License*: Public Domain *Contributors*: 84user, Jed, Quistnix, Rcbutcher, Saperaud

Image:Zeppelin wreck 23 sept 1916.JPG *Source*: http://en.wikipedia.org/w/index.php?title=File:Zeppelin_wreck_23_sept_1916.JPG *License*: Public Domain *Contributors*: Quistnix, Rcbutcher, Saperaud, Siebrand

File:LZ 104.jpg *Source*: http://en.wikipedia.org/w/index.php?title=File:LZ_104.jpg *License*: Public Domain *Contributors*: Original uploader was Zp at cs.wikipedia

Image:Airship Bodensee, Oct. 1919.jpg *Source*: http://en.wikipedia.org/w/index.php?title=File:Airship_Bodensee,_Oct._1919.jpg *License*: Public Domain *Contributors*: Hadhuey, Quistnix, Saperaud, Svencb

Image:LZ121 Nordstern.jpg *Source*: http://en.wikipedia.org/w/index.php?title=File:LZ121_Nordstern.jpg *License*: Public Domain *Contributors*: Denniss, Hadhuey, Saperaud

Image:ZR3 USS Los Angeles upright.jpg *Source*: http://en.wikipedia.org/w/index.php?title=File:ZR3_USS_Los_Angeles_upright.jpg *License*: Public Domain *Contributors*: Jutta234, Ogre, PMG, Quistnix, Saperaud, Van helsing

Image:Hindenburg at lakehurst.jpg *Source*: http://en.wikipedia.org/w/index.php?title=File:Hindenburg_at_lakehurst.jpg *License*: Public Domain *Contributors*: USN

VDM publishing house ltd.

Scientific Publishing House
offers
free of charge publication

of current academic research papers, Bachelor´s Theses, Master's Theses, Dissertations or Scientific Monographs

If you have written a thesis which satisfies high content as well as formal demands, and you are interested in a remunerated publication of your work, please send an e-mail with some initial information about yourself and your work to *info@vdm-publishing-house.com.*

Our editorial office will get in touch with you shortly.

VDM Publishing House Ltd.
Meldrum Court 17.
Beau Bassin
Mauritius
www.vdm-publishing-house.com

GNU Free Documentation License Version 1.2, November 2002

Copyright (C) 2000,2001,2002 Free Software Foundation, Inc. 59 Temple Place, Suite 330, Boston, MA 02111-1307 USA Everyone is permitted to copy and distribute verbatim copies of this license document, but changing it is not allowed.

0. PREAMBLE

The purpose of this License is to make a manual, textbook, or other functional and useful document "free" in the sense of freedom: to assure everyone the effective freedom to copy and redistribute it, with or without modifying it, either commercially or noncommercially. Secondarily, this License preserves for the author and publisher a way to get credit for their work, while not being considered responsible for modifications made by others.

This License is a kind of "copyleft", which means that derivative works of the document must themselves be free in the same sense. It complements the GNU General Public License, which is a copyleft license designed for free software. We have designed this License in order to use it for manuals for free software, because free software needs free documentation: a free program should come with manuals providing the same freedoms that the software does. But this License is not limited to software manuals; it can be used for any textual work, regardless of subject matter or whether it is published as a printed book. We recommend this License principally for works whose purpose is instruction or reference.

1. APPLICABILITY AND DEFINITIONS

This License applies to any manual or other work, in any medium, that contains a notice placed by the copyright holder saying it can be distributed under the terms of this License. Such a notice grants a world-wide, royalty-free license, unlimited in duration, to use that work under the conditions stated herein. The "Document", below, refers to any such manual or work. Any member of the public is a licensee, and is addressed as "you". You accept the license if you copy, modify or distribute the work in a way requiring permission under copyright law. A "Modified Version" of the Document means any work containing the Document or a portion of it, either copied verbatim, or with modifications and/or translated into another language.

A "Secondary Section" is a named appendix or a front-matter section of the Document that deals exclusively with the relationship of the publishers or authors of the Document to the Document's overall subject (or to related matters) and contains nothing that could fall directly within that overall subject. (Thus, if the Document is in part a textbook of mathematics, a Secondary Section may not explain any mathematics.) The relationship could be a matter of historical connection with the subject or with related matters, or of legal, commercial, philosophical, ethical or political position regarding them. The "Invariant Sections" are certain Secondary Sections whose titles are designated, as being those of Invariant Sections, in the notice that says that the Document is released under this License. If a section does not fit the above definition of Secondary then it is not allowed to be designated as Invariant. The Document may contain zero Invariant Sections. If the Document does not identify any Invariant Sections then there are none. The "Cover Texts" are certain short passages of text that are listed, as Front-Cover Texts or Back-Cover Texts, in the notice that says that the Document is released under this License. A Front-Cover Text may be at most 5 words, and a Back-Cover Text may be at most 25 words. A "Transparent" copy of the Document means a machine-readable copy, represented in a format whose specification is available to the general public, that is suitable for revising the document straightforwardly with generic text editors or (for images composed of pixels) generic paint programs or (for drawings) some widely available drawing editor, and that is suitable for input to text formatters or for automatic translation to a variety of formats suitable for input to text formatters. A copy made in an otherwise Transparent file format whose markup, or absence of markup, has been arranged to thwart or discourage subsequent modification by readers is not Transparent. An image format is not Transparent if used for any substantial amount of text. A copy that is not "Transparent" is called "Opaque". Examples of suitable formats for Transparent copies include plain ASCII without markup, Texinfo input format, LaTeX input format, SGML or XML using a publicly available DTD, and standard-conforming simple HTML, PostScript or PDF designed for human modification. Examples of transparent image formats include PNG, XCF and JPG. Opaque formats include proprietary formats that can be read and edited only by proprietary word processors, SGML or XML for which the DTD and/or processing tools are not generally available, and the machine-generated HTML, PostScript or PDF produced by some word processors for output purposes only. The "Title Page" means, for a printed book, the title page itself, plus such following pages as are needed to hold, legibly, the material this License requires to appear in the title page. For works in formats which do not have any title page as such, "Title Page" means the text near the most prominent appearance of the work's title, preceding the beginning of the body of the text. A section "Entitled XYZ" means a named subunit of the Document whose title either is precisely XYZ or contains XYZ in parentheses following text that translates XYZ in another language. (Here XYZ stands for a specific section name mentioned below, such as "Acknowledgements", "Dedications", "Endorsements", or "History".) To "Preserve the Title" of such a section when you modify the Document means that it remains a section "Entitled XYZ" according to this definition. The Document may include Warranty Disclaimers next to the notice which states that this License applies to the Document. These Warranty Disclaimers are considered to be included by reference in this License, but only as regards disclaiming warranties: any other implication that these Warranty Disclaimers may have is void and has no effect on the meaning of this License.

2. VERBATIM COPYING

You may copy and distribute the Document in any medium, either commercially or noncommercially, provided that this License, the copyright notices, and the license notice saying this License applies to the Document are reproduced in all copies, and that you add no other conditions whatsoever to those of this License. You may not use technical measures to obstruct or control the reading or further copying of the copies you make or distribute. However, you may accept compensation in exchange for copies. If you distribute a large enough number of copies you must also follow the conditions in section 3. You may also lend copies, under the same conditions stated above, and you may publicly display copies.

3. COPYING IN QUANTITY

If you publish printed copies (or copies in media that commonly have printed covers) of the Document, numbering more than 100, and the Document's license notice requires Cover Texts, you must enclose the copies in covers that carry, clearly and legibly, all these Cover Texts: Front-Cover Texts on the front cover, and Back-Cover Texts on the back cover. Both covers must also clearly and legibly identify you as the publisher of these copies. The front cover must present the full title with all words of the title equally prominent and visible. You may add other material on the covers in addition. Copying with changes limited to the covers, as long as they preserve the title of the Document and satisfy these conditions, can be treated as verbatim copying in other respects. If the required texts for either cover are too voluminous to fit legibly, you should put the first ones listed (as many as fit reasonably) on the actual cover, and continue the rest onto adjacent pages. If you publish or distribute Opaque copies of the Document numbering more than 100, you must either include a machine-readable Transparent copy along with each Opaque copy, or state in or with each Opaque copy a computer-network location from which the general network-using public has access to download using public-standard network protocols a complete Transparent copy of the Document, free of added material. If you use the latter option, you must take reasonably prudent steps, when you begin distribution of Opaque copies in quantity, to ensure that this Transparent copy will remain thus accessible at the stated location until at least one year after the last time you distribute an Opaque copy (directly or through your agents or retailers) of that edition to the public. It is requested, but not required, that you contact the authors of the Document well before redistributing any large number of copies, to give them a chance to provide you with an updated version of the Document.

4. MODIFICATIONS

You may copy and distribute a Modified Version of the Document under the conditions of sections 2 and 3 above, provided that you release the Modified Version under precisely this License, with the Modified Version filling the role of the Document, thus licensing distribution and modification of the Modified Version to whoever possesses a copy of it. In addition, you must do these things in the Modified Version: A. Use in the Title Page (and on the covers, if any) a title distinct from that of the Document, and from those of previous versions (which should, if there were any, be listed in the History section of the Document). You may use the same title as a previous version if the original publisher of that version gives permission. B. List on the Title Page, as authors, one or more persons or entities responsible for authorship of the modifications in the Modified Version, together with at least five of the principal authors of the Document (all of its principal authors, if it has fewer than five), unless they release you from this requirement. C. State on the Title page the name of the publisher of the Modified Version, as the publisher. D. Preserve all the copyright notices of the Document. E. Add an appropriate copyright notice for your modifications adjacent to the other copyright notices. F. Include, immediately after the copyright notices, a license notice giving the public permission to use the Modified Version under the terms of this License, in the form shown in the Addendum below. G. Preserve in that license notice the full lists of Invariant Sections and required Cover Texts given in the Document's license notice. H. Include an unaltered copy of this License. I. Preserve the section Entitled "History", Preserve its Title, and add to it an item stating at least the title, year, new authors, and publisher of the Modified Version as given on the Title Page. If there is no section Entitled "History" in the Document, create one stating the title, year, authors, and publisher of the Document as given on its Title Page, then add an item describing the Modified Version as stated in the previous sentence. J. Preserve the network location, if any, given in the Document for public access to a Transparent copy of the Document, and likewise the network locations given in the Document for previous versions it was based on. These may be placed in the "History" section. You may omit a network location for a work that was published at least four years before the Document itself, or if the original publisher of the version it refers to gives permission. K. For any section Entitled "Acknowledgements" or "Dedications", Preserve the Title of the section, and preserve in the section all the substance and tone of each of the contributor acknowledgements and/or dedications given therein. L. Preserve all the Invariant Sections of the Document, unaltered in their text and in their titles. Section numbers or the equivalent are not considered part of the section titles. M. Delete any section Entitled "Endorsements". Such a section may not be included in the Modified Version. N. Do not retitle any existing section to be Entitled "Endorsements" or to conflict in title with any Invariant Section. O. Preserve any Warranty Disclaimers. If the Modified Version includes new front-matter sections or appendices that qualify as Secondary Sections and contain no material copied from the Document, you may at your option designate some or all of these sections as invariant. To do this, add their titles to the list of Invariant Sections in the Modified Version's license notice. These titles must be distinct from any other section titles. You may add a section Entitled "Endorsements", provided it contains nothing but endorsements of your Modified Version by various parties--for example, statements of peer review or that the text has been approved by an organization as the authoritative definition of a standard. You may add a passage of up to five words as a Front-Cover Text, and a passage of up to 25 words as a Back-Cover Text, to the end of the list of Cover Texts in the Modified Version. Only one passage of Front-Cover Text and one of Back-Cover Text may be added by (or through arrangements made by) any one entity. If the Document already includes a cover text for the same cover, previously added by you or by arrangement made by the same entity you are acting on behalf of, you may not add another; but you may replace the old one, on explicit permission from the previous publisher that added the old one. The author(s) and publisher(s) of the Document do not by this License give permission to use their names for publicity for or to assert or imply endorsement of any Modified Version.

5. COMBINING DOCUMENTS

You may combine the Document with other documents released under this License, under the terms defined in section 4 above for modified versions, provided that you include in the combination all of the Invariant Sections of all of the original documents, unmodified, and list them all as Invariant Sections of your combined work in its license notice, and that you preserve all their Warranty Disclaimers. The combined work need only contain one copy of this License, and multiple identical Invariant Sections may be replaced with a single copy. If there are multiple Invariant Sections with the same name but different contents, make the title of each such section unique by adding at the end of it, in parentheses, the name of the original author or publisher of that section if known, or else a unique number. Make the same adjustment to the section titles in the list of Invariant Sections in the license notice of the combined work. In the combination, you must combine any sections Entitled "History" in the various original documents, forming one section Entitled "History"; likewise combine any sections Entitled "Acknowledgements", and any sections Entitled "Dedications". You must delete all sections Entitled "Endorsements".

6. COLLECTIONS OF DOCUMENTS

You may make a collection consisting of the Document and other documents released under this License, and replace the individual copies of this License in the various documents with a single copy that is included in the collection, provided that you follow the rules of this License for verbatim copying of each of the documents in all other respects. You may extract a single document from such a collection, and distribute it individually under this License, provided you insert a copy of this License into the extracted document, and follow this License in all other respects regarding verbatim copying of that document.

7. AGGREGATION WITH INDEPENDENT WORKS

A compilation of the Document or its derivatives with other separate and independent documents or works, in or on a volume of a storage or distribution medium, is called an "aggregate" if the copyright resulting from the compilation is not used to limit the legal rights of the compilation's users beyond what the individual works permit. When the Document is included in an aggregate, this License does not apply to the other works in the aggregate which are not themselves derivative works of the Document. If the Cover Text requirement of section 3 is applicable to these copies of the Document, then if the Document is less than one half of the entire aggregate, the Document's Cover Texts may be placed on covers that bracket the Document within the aggregate, or the electronic equivalent of covers if the Document is in electronic form. Otherwise they must appear on printed covers that bracket the whole aggregate.

8. TRANSLATION

Translation is considered a kind of modification, so you may distribute translations of the Document under the terms of section 4. Replacing Invariant Sections with translations requires special permission from their copyright holders, but you may include translations of some or all Invariant Sections in addition to the original versions of these Invariant Sections. You may include a translation of this License, and all the license notices in the Document, and any Warranty Disclaimers, provided that you also include the original English version of this License and the original versions of those notices and disclaimers. In case of a disagreement between the translation and the original version of this License or a notice or disclaimer, the original version will prevail. If a section in the Document is Entitled "Acknowledgements", "Dedications", or "History", the requirement (section 4) to Preserve its Title (section 1) will typically require changing the actual title.

9. TERMINATION

You may not copy, modify, sublicense, or distribute the Document except as expressly provided for under this License. Any other attempt to copy, modify, sublicense or distribute the Document is void, and will automatically terminate your rights under this License. However, parties who have received copies, or rights, from you under this License will not have their licenses terminated so long as such parties remain in full compliance.

10. FUTURE REVISIONS OF THIS LICENSE

The Free Software Foundation may publish new, revised versions of the GNU Free Documentation License from time to time. Such new versions will be similar in spirit to the present version, but may differ in detail to address new problems or concerns. See http://www.gnu.org/copyleft/. Each version of the License is given a distinguishing version number. If the Document specifies that a particular numbered version of this License "or any later version" applies to it, you have the option of following the terms and conditions either of that specified version or of any later version that has been published (not as a draft) by the Free Software Foundation. If the Document does not specify a version number of this License, you may choose any version ever published (not as a draft) by the Free Software Foundation.

ADDENDUM: How to use this License for your documents To use this License in a document you have written, include a copy of the License in the document and put the following copyright and license notices just after the title page: Copyright (c) YEAR YOUR NAME. Permission is granted to copy, distribute and/or modify this document under the terms of the GNU Free Documentation License, Version 1.2 or any later version published by the Free Software Foundation; with no Invariant Sections, no Front-Cover Texts, and no Back-Cover Texts. A copy of the license is included in the section entitled "GNU Free Documentation License". If you have Invariant Sections, Front-Cover Texts and Back-Cover Texts, replace the "with...Texts." line with this: with the Invariant Sections being LIST THEIR TITLES, with the Front-Cover Texts being LIST, and with the Back-Cover Texts being LIST. If you have Invariant Sections without Cover Texts, or some other combination of the three, merge those two alternatives to suit the situation. If your document contains nontrivial examples of program code, we recommend releasing these examples in parallel under your choice of free software license, such as the GNU General Public License, to permit their use in free software.

Lightning Source UK Ltd.
Milton Keynes UK
UKOW050448050512

192084UK00001B/34/P